STRATEGIC RESEARCH AGENDA FOR MULTILINGUAL EUROPE 2020

presented by the
META Technology Council

Editors
Georg Rehm
DFKI
Alt-Moabit 91c
Berlin 10559
Germany
e-mail: georg.rehm@dfki.de

Hans Uszkoreit
DFKI
Alt-Moabit 91c
Berlin 10559
Germany
e-mail: hans.uszkoreit@dfki.de

ISSN 2194-1416   ISSN 2194-1424   (electronic)
ISBN 978-3-642-36348-1   ISBN 978-3-642-36349-8   (eBook)
DOI 10.1007/978-3-642-36349-8
Springer Heidelberg New York Dordrecht London

Library of Congress Control Number: 2013931181

Printed on acid-free paper

Springer is part of Springer Science+Business Media (www.springer.com)

What are the major topics?

- *Information access and management.* Example: Information retrieval.
- *Communication between humans and between humans and machines.* Example: Spoken dialogue system.
- *Translation of spoken and written content.* Example: Document translation.

What are common Language Technology applications?

Language technologies include: spelling and grammar checkers; web search; voice dialing; interactive dialogue systems (e. g., phone banking or train reservation systems); interactive assistants such as Apple's Siri or Google's voice search; crosslingual search in digital libraries (e. g., Europeana); term extraction; speech synthesis for navigation systems; recommender systems for online shops; automatic content summarisation; and machine translation systems such as Google Translate and Microsoft's Bing Translator.

What is Language Technology?

Language technologies are technologies for automatically analysing and generating the most complex information medium in our world, *human language*, in both its spoken and written forms (as well as sign language). These technologies are developed by experts involved in linguistics, computer science, computational linguistics and related disciplines [1, 2, 3, 4].

Strategic Research Agenda for Multilingual Europe 2020
Presented by the META Technology Council
Edited by Georg Rehm and Hans Uszkoreit
Version 1.0 (December 1, 2012)

The project META-NET (T4ME, Grant Agreement 249 119) has been partially funded with support from the European Commission. This publication reflects the views only of the authors, and the Commission cannot be held responsible for any use which may be made of the information contained therein.

EUROPEAN INSIGHTS AND OPINIONS

Latvia: "For such small languages like Latvian keeping up with the ever increasing pace of time and technological development is crucial. The only way to ensure future existence of our language is to provide its users with equal opportunities as the users of larger languages enjoy. Therefore being on the forefront of modern technologies is our opportunity." — Valdis Dombrovskis (Prime Minister of Latvia)

Denmark: "If we have the ambition to use the Danish language in the technological universe of the future, an effort must be made now to maintain and further develop the knowledge and expertise that we already have. Otherwise we run the risk that only people who are fluent in English will profit from the new generations of web, mobile and robot technology which are up and coming." — Sabine Kirchmeier-Andersen (Director of the Danish Language Council)

Portugal: "Language technology is of utmost importance for the consolidation of Portuguese as a language of global communication in the information society." — Pedro Passos Coelho (Prime Minister of Portugal)

Czech Republic: "META-NET brings a significant contribution to the technological support for languages of Europe and as such will play an indispensable role in the development of multilingual European culture and society." — Ivan Wilhelm (Deputy Minister for Education, Youth and Sport)

Greece: "Further support to language technologies safeguards the presence of Greek language and culture in the digital environment, while at the same time promoting development and fostering communication among citizens within the Information Society." — George Babiniotis (Minister of Education, Lifelong Learning and Religious Affairs)

European Commission: "Having worked on automatic media analysis for many years and in tens of languages, we are painfully aware of the lack of text analysis tools and resources in most languages. META-NET's analysis is very accurate. Language Technology is a key enabling ingredient for future generations of IT. Languages for which no tools and resources will exist soon will not participate in the next major technological developments." — Ralf Steinberger (Joint Research Centre, IPSC – GlobeSec – Open-Source Text Information Mining and Analysis, Ispra, Italy)

Germany: "Global communications are a significant success factor for a globally active company. Accordingly, their importance is steadily increasing with the increased globalisation and growing complexity of international business. In this context, the design of effective and efficient language management processes makes an important contribution. The development of language technologies already plays a decisive role today and will continue to do so in the future. META-NET makes a pivotal contribution in the area of reseach and maintenance of networks with developers and users of language technologies." — Johannes Bursch (Head of Corporate Language Management, Daimler AG)

Estonia: "If we do not implement the development plan for language technology or do not cooperate with other countries in the same direction, in the future Estonian will be marginalised in information society." — Development Plan of the Estonian Language 2011–2017

Finland: "Without languages we could not communicate. The META-NET network is a valuable support for a multilingual Europe." — Alexander Stubb (Minister for European Affairs and Foreign Trade)

Croatia: "Language technologies play a crucial role in showcasing the linguistic richness of Europe." — Milena Žic Fuchs (Fellow of the Croatian Academy of Sciences and Arts, Chair of the Standing Committee for the Humanities of the European Science Foundation)

France: "META-NET provides an invaluable contribution to the development of a genuine European strategy in support to multilingualism, based on existing technologies while encouraging the development of new innovative technologies." — Xavier North (Délégué Général à la Langue Française et aux Langues de France)

Malta: "The technology support for the Maltese language should serve our language to be continuously cultivated, used and placed on the same level as other languages." — Dolores Cristina (Minister for Education and Employment)

Lithuania: "Conserving Lithuanian for future generations is a responsibility of the whole of the European Union. How we proceed with developing information technology will pretty much determine the future of the Lithuanian language." — Andrius Kubilius (Prime Minister of the Republic of Lithuania)

Ireland: "Language technology is no longer a luxury for most European languages – it is now essential to their survival as viable means of expression across the whole range of areas from business to the arts, and this is as much the case for Irish as any other European language." — Ferdie Mac an Fhailigh (CEO, Foras na Gaeilge)

Hungary: "META-NET is making a significant contribution to innovation, research and development in Europe and to an effective implementation of the European idea." — Valéria Csépe (Deputy General Secretary of Hungarian Academy of Sciences)

Sweden: "High-quality language technology may be the most effective means of preserving the linguistic diversity of Europe. Being able to use all languages fully in modern society is a question of democracy. In this connection META-NET fulfils a central, even crucial, function." — Lena Ekberg (Swedish Language Council)

Luxembourg: "This is a European challenge of enormous importance!" — Roman Jansen-Winkeln (CTO, Belingoo Media Group)

Slovenia: "It is imperative that language technologies for Slovene are developed systematically if we want Slovene to flourish also in the future digital world." — Danilo Türk (President of the Republic of Slovenia)

Iceland: "Language technology is an essential tool in a variety of linguistic research, and supports the official Icelandic policy of promoting the national language in all aspects of communication." — Guðrún Kvaran (Chair of the Icelandic Language Council)

Spain: "I like the spirit of the agenda!" — Juanjo Bermudez (Founder, Lingua e-Solutions SL)

Netherlands and Flanders (Belgium): "It remains extremely important that citizens can use their native language in all circumstances, including when they deal with modern ICT and leisure devices. But usually English speaking people are the first to benefit from such an evolution. Not only does this pose a danger of reducing the overall functionality of a language (and an impoverishment of an entire culture), but also it threatens those groups in society that do not master the universal language. Therefore, R&D programmes that support the local language are needed. Also in the future, the Dutch Language Union will continue to emphasise this issue." — Linde van den Bosch (General Secretary of the Dutch Language Union, 2004–2012)

Sweden: "The Priority Research Themes hit the bull's eye. Let's all hope for the best for the report." — Jens Erik Rasmussen (New Business Manager, Mikro Værkstedet)

Romania: "Linguistic technologies represent a central element of the EU, because languages themselves occupy a central place in the functioning of the EU." — Leonard Orban (former European Commissioner for Multilingualism)

UK: "The work of META-NET is an important step towards a future in which Language Technology will be all around us, allowing us to collaborate, conduct business and share knowledge with friends and colleagues, whether or not we speak the same language." — David Willets (Minister of State for Universities and Science, Department for Business, Innovation and Skills)

Poland: "Language technologies are more and more present in our everyday life. For their presence to be rational and functional, for it to serve the needs of the economy, as well as the social and cultural life well, further large-scale work in this area is needed." — Michał Kleiber (President of the Polish Academy of Sciences)

Germany: "Europe's multilingualism and our scientific expertise are the perfect prerequisites for significantly advancing the challenge that language technology poses. META-NET opens up new opportunities for the development of ubiquitous multilingual technologies." — Annette Schavan (Minister of Education and Research)

See http://www.meta-net.eu/whitepapers/all-quotes-and-testimonials for additional quotes and testimonials.

"The Commission will [...] work with stakeholders to develop a new generation of web-based applications and services, including for multilingual content and services, by supporting standards and open platforms through EU-funded programmes." – *A Digital Agenda for Europe* [5], p. 24

"Everybody must have the chance to communicate efficiently in the enlarged EU. This does not only affect those who already are multilingual but also those who are monolingual or linguistically less skilled.

The media, new technologies and human and automatic translation services can bring the increasing variety of languages and cultures in the EU closer to citizens and provide the means to cross language barriers. They can also play an important role to reduce those barriers and allow citizens, companies and national administrations to exploit the opportunities of the single market and the globalising economy.

Faced with the globalising online economy and ever-increasing information in all imaginable languages, it is important that citizens access and use information and services across national and language barriers, through the internet and mobile devices. Information and communication technologies (ICT) need to be language-aware and promote content creation in multiple languages." – *Multilingualism: An Asset for Europe and a Shared Commitment* [6], p. 12 f.

"The Council of the European Union [...] encourage[s] the development of language technologies, in particular in the field of translation and interpretation, firstly by promoting cooperation between the Commission, the Member States, local authorities, research bodies and industry, and secondly by ensuring convergence between research programmes, the identification of areas of application and the deployment of the technologies across all EU languages." – *Council Resolution of 21 November 2008 on a European strategy for multilingualism* [7]

"The language of Europe is translation." – Umberto Eco (1993)

TABLE OF CONTENTS

KEY MESSAGES

European society is multilingual: the diversity of its cultural heritage is an asset and an opportunity.

- Europe is and will remain a multilingual, integrative and inclusive society. Geographical Europe has more than 80 languages, including the EU's 23 official languages as well as minority and immigrant languages.
- Languages without sufficient technological support will become marginalised and threatened by digital extinction.
- While decent technologies exist for English, Europe's other languages are under-supported, many of them seriously.

Language barriers must be overcome: language technology is a key enabler which will help solve this problem.

- Language barriers are hindering the free flow of information, goods, knowledge, thought and innovation.
- If the European community makes a dedicated push, we can get rid of many language barriers by 2020 and thus fully realise the single digital space and marketplace.
- Europeans will be able to communicate with one another, with their governments and with web services in their native mother tongue.

Language technology is a key enabling technology for the next IT revolution.

- The next revolution in IT will bring technology much closer to the human user.
- The next generation of IT will be able to handle human language, knowledge and emotion in meaningful ways.
- Language technology will enable a host of powerful innovative services in the exploitation of big data, in knowledge use and transmission, in the control of technology, in learning and in many other areas.
- After having missed some opportunities in the past, Europe still has a splendid chance to become a leading actor and economic beneficiary of this revolution.
- The problem in Europe is the lack of take-up by industry because research and innovation funding in LT has fallen short of the scale, coordination and breath needed to drive the ball into the goal.

By a focused, concerted, major interdisciplinary LT research effort, Europe can preserve its precious languages, benefit from language diversity and from existing strengths and play a leading role in the next IT revolution.

- This SRA outlines three priority themes with ambitious research goals, powerful applications and first indicative roadmaps: Translingual Cloud; Social Intelligence and e-Participation; Socially Aware Interactive Assistants.
- A needed horizontal effort across the priority themes is the coordinated development, improvement and sharing of indispensable base technologies and resources for all European languages.
- A cloud platform is proposed for providing free and commercial language technology services including the access to a wealth of public and private web-services in any European language.
- The massive push needs to be accompanied by policy making such as regulations supporting the multilingual setup of our society and the effective utilisation of language data for research and technology development.
- The proposed measures have the power to bring about a quantum leap in the evolution of IT, put Europe in a leading position in a core area of economic growth and to allow our languages to thrive in the digital age.

EXECUTIVE SUMMARY

The unique multilingual setup of our European society imposes grand societal challenges on political, economic and social integration and inclusion, especially in the creation of the single digital market and unified information space targeted by the Digital Agenda.

As many as 21 European languages are at risk of digital extinction. They could become victims of the digital age as they are under-represented online and under-resourced with respect to language techno–logies. Moreover, huge market opportunities remain untapped because of language barriers. If no action is taken, many European citizens will find that speaking their mother tongue leaves them at a social and economic disadvantage. Future-proofing our languages requires a modest investment which will return a strong competitive advantage, since the technologies needed to overcome language barriers and support languages in the digital age are key enabling technologies for the next IT revolution.

Language technology is the missing piece of the puzzle that will bring us closer to a single digital market. Almost every digital product uses and is dependent on language – this is why language technology is not an option! It is the key enabler and solution to boosting future growth in Europe and strengthening our competitiveness in a technology sector that is becoming increasingly important. The key question is: Will Europe wholeheartedly decide to participate in this fast growing market?

Although we use computers to write, phones to chat and the web to search for knowledge, IT does not yet have access to the meaning, purpose and sentiment behind our trillions of written and spoken words. Technology will bridge the rift separating IT and the human mind using sophisticated technologies for language understanding. Recent language technology innovations such as Google's web search, Autonomy's text analytics, Nuance's speech tools, online translation services, IBM Watson's question answering and Apple's Siri have given us but a first glimpse of the massive potential behind this important emerging technology. Today's computers cannot understand texts and questions well enough to provide translations, summaries or reliable answers, but in less than ten years such services will be offered for many languages. Technological mastery of human language will enable a host of innovative IT products and services in commerce, administration, government, education, health care, entertainment, tourism and other sectors.

Europe is the most appropriate place for accomplishing the needed breakthroughs in fundamental and applied research and technology evolution. Our continent has half a billion citizens who speak one of over 60 European and many non-European languages as their mother tongue. Europe has more than 2,500 small and medium sized enterprises in language, knowledge and interface technologies, and more than 5,000 enterprises providing language services that can be improved and extended by technology. In addition, it has a long-standing R&D tradition with over 800 centres performing scientific and technological research on all European and many non-European languages.

Europe's language technology community is dedicated to fulfilling the requirements of our multilingual society and turning its needs and business opportunities into competitive advantages for our economy. Recognising Europe's exceptional demand and opportunities, 60 leading IT research centres in 34 European countries joined forces in META-NET, a European Network of Excellence dedicated to the technological foundations of a multilingual, inclusive, innovative and reflective European society and partially supported through several EC-funded projects.

META-NET assembled the Multilingual Europe Technology Alliance (META) with more than 650 organisations and experts representing stakeholders such as industries that provide or use language technologies, research organisations, professional associations, public administrations and language communities. Working together with numerous additional stakeholder organisations and experts from a variety of fields, META/META-NET has developed this Strategic Research Agenda (SRA). Our recommendations for Multilingual Europe 2020, as specified in this document, are based on a thorough planning process involving more than one thousand experts.

The META Technology Council predicts, in line with many other forecasts, that the next generation of IT will be able to handle human language, knowledge and emotion in competent and meaningful ways. These new competencies will enable an endless stream of novel services that will improve communication and understanding. Many services will help people learn about and understand things such as world history, technology, nature and the economy. Others will help us to better understand each other across language and knowledge boundaries. They will also drive many other services including programmes for commerce, localisation, personal assistance, and allow robots to understand what their users want and need.

Our ultimate goal is monolingual, crosslingual and multilingual technology support for all languages spoken by a significant population in Europe. To achieve this, we recommend focusing on a small set of selected priority research topics dedicated to innovative application scenar-

ios that will provide European research and development in this field with the ability to compete with other markets and subsequently achieve multiple benefits for European society and citizens as well as an array of opportunities for our economy and future growth. We are confident that upcoming EU funding programmes, specifically Horizon 2020 and Connecting Europe Facility, combined with national and regional funding, can provide the necessary resources for accomplishing our joint vision.

A recent policy brief by the Bruegel think tank proposes that Europe specialises in new ICT sectors as a means for post-crisis recovery. The European problem lies less in the generation of new ideas than in their successful commercialisation, and the study identifies the major obstacles: the lack of a single digital market, and the absence of ICT clusters and powerful platform providers. It suggests that the EU policy framework could overcome these barriers and leverage the growth potential of new ICT markets by extending research and infrastructure funding to precommercial projects, in particular those involving the creation of ICT clusters and platforms. This is exactly the goal we are trying to achieve with this SRA in our IT sector. Our recommendations envisage five lines of action for large-scale research and innovation:

- **Three Priority Research Themes** along with powerful application scenarios to drive research and innovation. These will demonstrate novel technologies in show-case solutions with high economic and societal impact and creating numerous new business opportunities for European companies.

  1. **Translingual Cloud**: generic and specialised federated cloud services for reliable spoken and written translation among all European and major non-European languages.

  2. **Social Intelligence and e-Participation**: understanding and dialogue within and across communities of citizens, customers, clients and consumers to enable e-participation and establish more effec-

tive processes for preparing, selecting and evaluating collective decisions.

3. **Socially Aware Interactive Assistants**: socially aware pervasive assistants that learn and adapt and provide proactive and interactive support tailored to the specific situations, locations and goals of the user by means of verbal and non-verbal multimodal communication.

- The other two themes focus upon base technologies and a platform for services and technologies:

4. **Core technologies and resources for Europe's languages**: a system of shared, collectively maintained, interoperable tools and resources. They will ensure that our languages will be sufficiently supported and represented in future generations of IT solutions.

5. **European service platform for language technologies** for supporting research and innovation by testing and showcasing results, integrating research and operational services, including professional human services. This e-infrastructure will allow providers from research and industry to offer components and services.

The objective of the priority research themes is to turn our joint vision into reality and allow Europe to benefit from a technological revolution that will overcome barriers of understanding between people of different languages, people and technology, and people and the digitised knowledge of mankind.

The themes respond to societal needs using LT-based solutions and provide concrete roadmaps for the planning of research, development and scientific innovation. They cover the main functions of language: storing, sharing and using information and knowledge; improving social interaction among humans; enabling social interaction between humans and technology. As multilingualism is at the heart of European culture and is increasingly becoming a global norm, one of the themes is devoted to overcoming language barriers.

The SRA recommends ways in which research and innovation need to be organised in order to achieve the targeted research breakthroughs and benefit from the immense economic opportunities they create. Core components of the strategy are innovative modes of large-scale collective research and interaction among the major stakeholder constituencies, including researchers in several disciplines, technology providers, technology users, policy makers and language communities.

It is decisive that intermediate results are quickly and effectively converted to solutions that will have a societal and economic impact and contribute to the rewarding practice of technological, social and cultural innovation as set out in the Digital Agenda as well as Horizon 2020 and Connecting Europe Facility (CEF).

1

INTRODUCTION

During the last 60 years, Europe has become a distinct political and economic structure. Culturally and linguistically it is rich and diverse. However, from Portuguese to Polish and Italian to Icelandic, everyday communication between Europe's citizens, enterprises and politicians is inevitably confronted with language barriers. They are an invisible and increasingly problematic threat to economic growth as several recent studies have shown [8].

The EU's institutions spend about *one billion Euros per year* on translation and interpretation to maintain their policy of multilingualism [9] and the overall European market for translation, interpretation, software localisation and website globalisation was estimated at 5.7 billion Euros in 2008. Are these expenses necessary? Are they even sufficient? Despite this high level of expenditure, only a fraction of the information is translated that is available to the whole population in countries with a single predominant language, such as the USA or China.

Language technology and linguistic research, as well as related fields such as the digital humanities, social sciences and psychology, can significantly contribute to overcoming linguistic barriers. Combined with intelligent devices and applications, a European language technology platform will help European citizens to talk and do business together even if they do not speak a mutual language.

The economy benefits from the European single market. But language barriers can bring business to a halt, especially for SMEs who do not have the financial means to compete on a European or global level. The only (unacceptable) alternative to a multilingual Europe [10] would be to allow a single language to take a predominant position and replace all other languages in transnational communication. Another way to overcome language barriers is to learn foreign languages, an area in which language technologies can play a key role.

Given the 23 official EU languages plus 60 or more other languages spoken in Europe [11], language learning on its own cannot solve the problem of cross-border communication or commerce [8]. Without technological support such as machine translation, our linguistic diversity will be an insurmountable obstacle for the entire continent. Only about half of the 500 million people who live in the European Union speak English! It is evident that there is no such thing as a lingua franca shared by the vast majority of the population of our continent.

Less than 10% of the EU's population are willing or able to use online services in English which is why multilingual services based on language technologies are badly needed to support and to move the EU online market from more than 20 language-specific sub-markets to a unified single digital market with more than 500 million users and consumers. The main goal, foreseen in the Digital Agenda EU policy framework [5], is to build a single digital market in which content and services can flow freely. In order to support cross-border exchanges between users, consumers, countries and regions [8], robust and high-quality cross- and multilingual language technologies need to be developed urgently. In fact, the current situation with "many fragmented markets" is considered one of the main obstacles that seriously undermine Europe's efforts to exploit ICT fully [5]! A truly functioning single digital market can only be established once

G. Rehm and H. Uszkoreit (eds.), *META-NET Strategic Research Agenda for Multilingual Europe 2020*, White Paper Series, DOI: 10.1007/978-3-642-36349-8_1, © The Author(s) 2013

the language barrier has fallen, something that can be achieved only through research, development and wide deployment of language technologies (see Figure 1). The single digital market functions poorly because multilingual Europe itself functions poorly.

Language technology is a key enabler for sustainable, cost-effective and socially beneficial solutions to overcome language barriers. It will offer European stakeholders tremendous advantages, not only within the European market, but also in trade relations with non-European countries, especially emerging economies. One prerequisite to develop these solutions was a systematic survey of the linguistic particularities of all European languages and the current state of language technology support for them. With the publication of the META-NET White Paper Series "Europe's Languages in the Digital Age" [12] this important step has now been taken (see also Chapter 4, p. 27 ff., and Appendix C, p. 80 for an overview of the timeline and history of this document).

There are two main axes around which language technologies are needed and able to bring about the next IT revolution: *communication* and *data analysis*. Communication includes support for activities such as talking, conversing, carrying out dialogues and debates (both spoken and written), authoring and further processing (summarising, categorising etc.) of texts ranging from instant messages to complex documents, and also translation. Data analysis includes organising, structuring and understanding data, extracting information and relations between entities. The term data here refers to arbitrary types of unstructured data as well as any type of text. In the medium-to-long term we want to realise technologies for socially-aware and context-aware natural language understanding and generation, including translation.

In the late 1970s the EU realised the profound relevance of language technology as a driver of European unity and began funding its first research projects, such as EURO-TRA. After a longer period of sparse funding [13, 14],

the European Commission set up a department dedicated to language technology and machine translation a few years ago; in an internal reorganisation this department was recently integrated into a new unit called "Data Value Chain", part of Directorate G, "Media & Data", in the EC Directorate General for "Communications Networks, Content and Technology" (DG Connect). In the past ca. five years, the EU has been supporting projects such as EuroMatrix and EuroMatrix+ (since 2006) and iTranslate4 (since 2010), which use basic and applied research to generate resources for establishing high-quality solutions for all European languages.

These selective funding efforts have led to a number of valuable results. For example, the EC's translation services now use the Moses open source machine translation software, which has been mainly developed in European research projects. However, these projects never led to a concerted European effort through which the EU and its member states systematically pursue the common goal of providing technology support for all European languages. Figure 2 depicts the languages that have been studied by Language Technology researchers in 2010, taking into account major conferences and journals. It illustrates how research has focussed primarily on English followed by Chinese, German, French, and a few other bigger languages. Many European languages were not studied at all, e. g., Slovak, Maltese, Lithuanian, Irish, Albanian, Croatian, Macedonian, Montenegrin, Romansh, Galician, Occitan, or Frisian.

Research activities have tended to be isolated and while they have delivered valuable results, they have had difficulty making a decisive impact on the market. In many cases research funded in Europe eventually bore fruit outside Europe; enterprises such as Google and Apple have been noteworthy beneficiaries. In fact, many of the predominant actors in the field today are based in the US.

Europe now has a well-developed research base. Through initiatives such as CLARIN and META-NET the re-

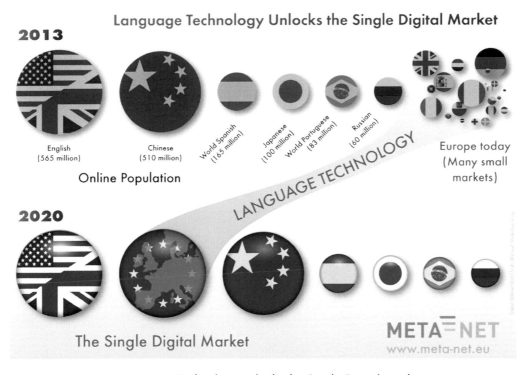

Language Technology Unlocks the Single Digital Market

2013

English (565 million)
Chinese (510 million)
World Spanish (165 million)
Japanese (100 million)
World Portuguese (83 million)
Russian (60 million)
Europe today (Many small markets)

Online Population

2020

LANGUAGE TECHNOLOGY

The Single Digital Market

META-NET
www.meta-net.eu

1: Language Technology unlocks the Single Digital Market

search community is well connected and engaged in a long term agenda that aims gradually to strengthen language technology's role. At the same time, our position is worse when compared to other multilingual societies. Despite having fewer financial resources, countries like India (22 official languages) and South Africa (11 official languages) have set up long-term national programmes for language research and technology development. What is missing in Europe is awareness, political determination and political will that would take us to a leading position in this technology area through a concerted funding effort. This major dedicated push needs to include the political determination to modify and to adopt a shared, EU-wide language policy that foresees an important role for language technologies.

Drawing on the insights gained so far, today's hybrid language technology mixing deep processing with statistical methods could be able to bridge the gap between all European languages and beyond. In the end, high-quality language technology will be a must for all of Europe's languages for supporting the political and economic unity through cultural diversity. Language technology can help tear down existing barriers and build bridges between Europe's languages. In the digital age, communication with people and machines, as well as the unrestricted access to the knowledge of the world should be possible for all languages. The European LT community is dedicated to fulfilling the technology demands of the multilingual European society and to turn these needs and emerging business opportunities into competitive advantages. To this end, we have developed this Strategic Research Agenda (see Appendix C, p. 80)

In the first chapters we analyse the multilingual technology needs arising from the multicultural setup of our continent with its emerging single digital market. We also discuss the current state of technologies for European languages. The two core chapters of this document summarise our shared vision of the role of language technol-

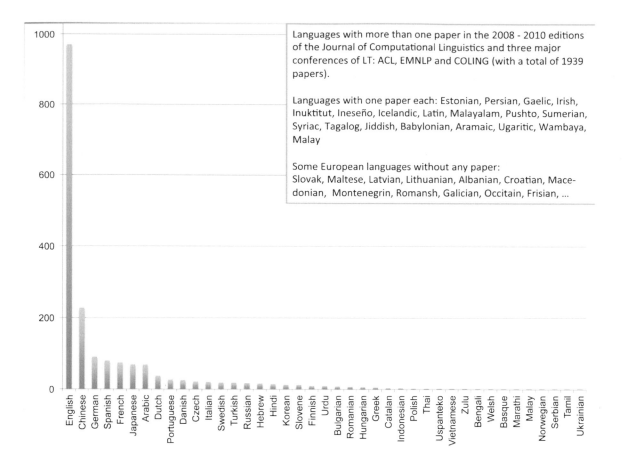

Languages with more than one paper in the 2008 - 2010 editions of the Journal of Computational Linguistics and three major conferences of LT: ACL, EMNLP and COLING (with a total of 1939 papers).

Languages with one paper each: Estonian, Persian, Gaelic, Irish, Inuktitut, Ineseño, Icelandic, Latin, Malayalam, Pushto, Sumerian, Syriac, Tagalog, Jiddish, Babylonian, Aramaic, Ugaritic, Wambaya, Malay

Some European languages without any paper:
Slovak, Maltese, Latvian, Lithuanian, Albanian, Croatian, Macedonian, Montenegrin, Romansh, Galician, Occitain, Frisian, ...

2: Languages treated in research published in the 2008–2010 edition of the Journal of Computational Linguistics and the conferences of ACL, EMNLP and COLING (internal, unpublished study)

ogy in the year 2020 in non-technical terms (Chapter 5, p. 32 ff.) and outline three priority themes for large-scale research and innovation (Chapter 6, p. 41 ff.):

1. **Translingual Cloud** – Services for instantaneous reliable spoken and written translation among all European and major non-European languages

2. **Social Intelligence and e-Participation** – understanding and dialogue within and across communities of citizens, customers, clients, consumers

3. **Socially Aware Interactive Assistants** – analysis and synthesis of non-verbal, speech and semantic signals

These thematic directions have been designed with the aim of turning our joint vision into reality and to letting Europe benefit from a technological revolution that will overcome barriers of understanding between people of different languages, between people and technology and between people and the accumulated knowledge of mankind. The themes build the bridge between societal needs, applications, and roadmaps for the organisation of research, development and scientific innovation. They cover the main functions of language: storing, sharing and using information and knowledge, as well as improving social interaction among humans and enabling social interaction between humans and technology.

We also present ways in which research and innovation need to be organised in order to achieve the targeted breakthroughs and to benefit from the immense economic opportunities they create. Core components of the sketched strategy are novel modes of large-scale collective research and interaction among the major stakeholder constituencies including research in several disciplines, technology providers, technology users, policy makers and language communities. Effective schemes for sharing resources such as data, computational language models and generic base technologies are also an integral part of our strategy. Of central importance is a rapid flow of intermediate results into commercially viable solutions of societal impact contributing to the fertile culture of technological, social and cultural innovation targeted by the Digital Agenda [5] and the programmes Connecting Europe Facility (CEF) [15] and Horizon 2020 [16].

The three priority research themes are mainly aimed at Horizon 2020 (2014–2020). The more infrastructural aspects, platform design and implementation and concrete language technology services are aimed at CEF. Our suggestion for integrating multilingual technologies into the wider CEF framework is to develop innovative solutions that enable providers of online services to offer their content and services in as many EU languages as possible, in a most cost effective way. These are to include public services, commercial services and user-generated con-

tent. An integral component of our strategic plans are the member states and associated countries: it is of utmost importance to set up, under the overall umbrella of our SRA and priority research themes, a coordinated initiative both on the national (member states, regions, associated countries) and international level (EC/EU), including research centres as well as small, medium and large enterprises who work on or with language technologies. Only through an agreement and update of our national and international language policy frameworks, close cooperation between all stakeholders, and tightly coordinated collaboration can we realise the ambituous plan of researching, designing, developing and putting into practice a European platform [17] that supports all citizens of Europe, and beyond, by providing, among others, sophisticated services for communication across language barriers.

MULTILINGUAL EUROPE: FACTS, CHALLENGES, OPPORTUNITIES

2.1 EUROPE'S LANGUAGES IN THE NETWORKED SOCIETY

Europe's more than 80 languages are one of its richest and most important cultural assets, and a vital part of its unique social model [6, 11]. While languages such as English and Spanish are likely to thrive in the emerging digital marketplace, many European languages could become marginal in a networked society. This would weaken Europe's global standing, and run counter to the goal of ensuring equal participation for every European citizen regardless of language. A recent UNESCO report on multilingualism states that languages are an essential medium for the enjoyment of fundamental rights, such as political expression, education and participation in society [18, 19, 20, 21]. From the very beginning, Europe had decided to keep its cultural and linguistic richness and diversity alive during the process of becoming an economic and political union. For maintaining the policy of multilingualism, the EU's institutions spend about one billion Euros a year on translating texts and interpreting spoken communication. For all European economies the translation costs for compliance with the laws and regulations are much higher.

A single European market that secures wealth and social well-being is possible, but linguistic barriers still severely limit the free flow of goods, information, services, debates and innovation. With the increased number of EU members and the general trend towards timely trans-border interaction, everyday communication between Europe's citizens, within business and among politicians is more and more becoming confronted with language barriers. Many Europeans find it difficult to interact with online services and participate in the digital economy. According to a recent study, 57% of internet users in Europe purchase goods and services in languages that are not their native language (English is the most common foreign language followed by French, German and Spanish). 55% of users read content in a foreign language while only 35% use another language to write e-mails or post comments on the web [22]. A few years ago, English might have been the lingua franca of the web – the vast majority of content on the web was in English – but the situation has now drastically changed. The amount of online content in other European as well as Asian and Middle Eastern languages has exploded [23]. Already today, more than 55% of web-based content is not in English. One language is especially becoming more and more dominant: a recent study by the UN Broadband Commission reports that Chinese internet users will overtake English language users by 2015 [24].

Figure 3 shows the European language communities of Twitter: the map was created by identifying automatically the languages millions of tweets are written in and placing them onto a map using their GPS-coordinates [25]. To a large degree the resulting map replicates Europe's language borders – and barriers.

Surprisingly, this ubiquitous digital divide due to language borders and language barriers has not gained much

G. Rehm and H. Uszkoreit (eds.), *META-NET Strategic Research Agenda for Multilingual Europe 2020*,
 White Paper Series, DOI: 10.1007/978-3-642-36349-8_2, © The Author(s) 2013

English
Portuguese
Indonesian
Spanish
Malay
Japanese
Dutch
Korean
Filipino
Russian
French
Thai
Italian
German
Turkish
Arabic
Swedish
Danish
Finnish
Catalan
Chinese
Romanian
Norwegian
Lithuanian
Slovak
Czech
Vietnamese
Greek
Hungarian
Polish
Afrikaans
Slovenian
Albanian
Latvian
Chinese (TW)
Galician
Swahili
Hebrew
Croatian
Bulgarian

3: Language communities of Twitter (European detail) [25]

public attention up until our recent press campaign in which we informed the public about the findings of our META-NET study "Europe's Languages in the Digital Age" (see Chapter 4, p. 27 ff.). In this study, published in our META-NET White Paper Series [12], more than 200 experts from all over Europe found that at least 21 of the 30 languages examined are in serious danger of facing digital extinction. A pressing question raises: which European languages will thrive in the networked information society, and which are doomed to disappear?

The European market for translation, interpretation and localisation was estimated to be 5.7 billion Euros in 2008. The subtitling and dubbing sector was at 633 million Eu-

ros, language teaching at 1.6 billion Euros. The overall value of the European language industry was estimated at 8.4 billion Euros and expected to grow by 10% per year, i. e., resulting in ca. 16.5 billion Euros in 2015 [26, 27]. (The global speech technology market is even bigger, it will reach ca. 20.9 billion US-Dollars by 2015 and ca. 31.3 billion US-Dollars by 2017 [28].) Yet, this existing capacity is not enough to satisfy current and future needs, e. g., with regard to translation [29]. Already today, Google Translate translates the same volume per day that all human translators on the planet translate in one year [30].

Despite recent improvements, the quality, usability and integration of machine translation into other online services is far from what is needed. If we rely on existing technologies, automated translation and the ability to process a variety of content in a variety of languages – a key requirement for the future internet – will be impossible. The same applies to information services, document services, media industries, digital archives and language teaching. There is an urgent need for innovative technologies that help save costs while offering faster and better language services to the European citizen.

The most compelling solution for ensuring the breadth and depth of language usage in tomorrow's Europe is to use appropriate technology. Still, despite recent improvements, the quality and usability of current technologies is far from what is needed. The META-NET study mentioned above shows that, already today, especially the smaller European languages suffer severely from underrepresentation in the digital realm. There are tremendous deficits in technology support and significant research gaps for all languages. For example, machine translation support for 23 out of the studied 30 languages was evaluated as having very limited quality and performance, which is an alarming result!

Another important aspect related to the European discourse. Especially the one on innovation has become determined by the English language, and the media reporting in that language. As Mark Vanderbeeken, a Belgian who lives in Italy noted in a widely read essay [31], this sheer dominance of English carries with it an accompanying perspective of Europe, both in terms of stereotypes and in terms of relevance to the Anglo-Saxon world. This puts European businesses and countries at a serious disadvantage that they are not even aware of. It also disadvantages businesses in the English-speaking world, which are perhaps not aware that they are receiving an abbreviated picture of innovation in Europe. Vanderbeeken calls this phenomenon "the non-English disadvantage". It is another example of a disadvantage which can be successfully addressed through multilingual technologies.

2.2 HOW CAN LANGUAGE TECHNOLOGY HELP?

One way to overcome language barriers is to learn foreign languages. Yet without technological support, mastering the EU's 23 official languages and some 60 other European languages is an insurmountable obstacle for Europe's citizens, economy, scientific progress, and political debate [32]. The solution is to build key enabling technologies: language technologies will offer all European stakeholders tremendous advantages and benefits, not only in the single market, but also in trade relations with non-European countries.

Language technology is also a key enabler for the knowledge society. It supports humans in everyday tasks, such as writing e-mails, searching for information online or booking a flight. It is often used behind the scenes of other software applications. We benefit when we use spelling checkers, browse recommendations in an online shop, hear the spoken instructions of a navigation system or translate web pages with an online service.

Several popular language technology services are provided by US companies, some of them free of charge. The recent success of Watson, an IBM computer system that won against human candidates in the game show Jeopardy, illustrates the immense potential. As Europeans, we urgently have to ask ourselves a few crucial questions:

- Can we afford our information, communication and knowledge infrastructure to be highly dependent upon monopolistic services provided by US companies (technological lock-in)?

- What is Europe's fallback plan in case the language-related services provided by US companies that we rely upon are suddenly switched off or if serious access or security issues arise?

- Are we actively making an effort to compete in the global landscape for research and development in language technology?

- Can we expect third parties from other continents to solve our translation and knowledge management problems in a way that suits our specific communicative, societal and cultural needs?

- Can the European cultural background help shape the knowledge society by offering better, more secure, more precise, more innovative and more robust high-quality language technology?

We believe that *Language Technology made in Europe for Europe* will significantly contribute to future European cross-border and cross-language communication, economic growth [8] and social stability while establishing for Europe a worldwide, leading position in technology innovation, securing Europe's future as a world-wide trader and exporter of goods, services and information.

2.3 SOCIETAL CHALLENGES

Information technology is bringing people speaking different languages together in new ways. Highly popular social networks and social media such as Wikipedia, Facebook, Twitter, YouTube, Google+, Pinterest, and Instagram are only the tip of the iceberg.

Many societal changes and economic as well as technological trends confirm the urgent need to include sophisticated language technology in our European ICT infrastructure. Research, development and innovation efforts in LT must increase to go beyond what is possible today.

Language Barriers. A study on online commerce shows that language barriers are economic barriers [33]. Only 59% of retailers can handle transactions in more than one language. Translation and localisation costs must be drastically lowered before Europe's single digital market is a reality. Multilingual language technology is the key, especially for SMEs. At the same time, 81% of all internet users think that websites run in their country should also be available in other languages. 44% of European users think they miss out on interesting information because

websites are not available in a language they understand [22]. These facts can no longer be ignored. Reliable LT can help establish a vast market for information as well as consumer and entertainment goods in any language.

Ageing Population. Demographic changes bring about a need for more assistive technologies, especially for spoken language access. An ageing population requires technology that can help master everyday situations, provide proactive guidance and that could answer the question, "Where did I leave my glasses?" Also, more health care services and support systems will be required. Ambient assisted living (AAL) technologies can greatly benefit from a personalised, spoken method of interaction.

People with Disabilities. New technologies can help us reach the ambitious goal of achieving equal opportunities and promoting independent living. Language technologies already help people with disabilities to participate in society. Noteworthy examples include screen readers, dictation systems and voice-activated services. In addition to the social aspect there is a huge commercial market for future technologies such as, for example, full dialogue systems and interactive assistants, sign language recognition and synthesis, automatic translation, summarisation and content simplification. Approximately 10% of Europeans (50 million citizens) have permanent disabilities.

Immigration and Integration. According to the United Nations' International Migration Report 2002, 56 million migrants lived in Europe in 2000 [34]. This number has grown to ca. 60 million people today. Facilitating communication, providing access to information in foreign languages and helping people learn European languages can help better integrate migrants into European society. In fact, speech and language technologies can dramatically improve the integration process by providing intelligent language learning environments, automatic subtitling and translation services in real time.

Personal Information Services and Customer Care. In our 24/7 "always on" economy we expect quick and reliable answers as well as engaging and timely online news broadcasts. However, information overload still poses a serious problem. Citizens, governments and industries would greatly benefit from new technologies that help get the situation under control again. Language-enabled mobile applications will become personal assistants to everyone, offering automatic and intelligent question answering and dialogue capabilities, as well as automatic, personalised and trusted text and speech processing of messages, news items and other content.

Global Cooperation and Human Communication. Companies need to address new markets where multiple languages are spoken and support multinational teams at multiple locations. Many jobs cannot be filled today because linguistic barriers exclude otherwise qualified personnel. Improvements in language technology can enable richer interactions and provide more advanced tele and video conferencing services. Future technologies like a 3D internet can enable new modes of collaboration as well as support more realistic training and education scenarios. We will soon be able to participate in virtual events as new forms of entertainment, cultural exchange and tourism. Combining virtual worlds and simulations with multilingual language technology including translation, automatic minute taking, video indexing and searching will let us experience being European in a new way.

Preservation of Cultural Heritage and Linguistic Diversity. According to the principles of the UN-endorsed World Summit on the Information Society [35], the "Information Society should be founded on and stimulate respect for cultural identity, cultural and linguistic diversity." Much effort has been put into digital archives such as Europeana that help promote our cultural heritage. However, digitisation is only the first step. The sheer amount of information and language barriers hinder access of our cultural treasures. Language technology can make this content accessible, e. g., through cross-lingual search and machine translation. Likewise, com-

munication skills need to be trained. This is underlined by the UNESCO Information for All Programme, which seeks to "foster the availability of indigenous knowledge through basic literacy and ICT literacy training" [36].

Social Media and e-Participation. Social networks have a significant impact on all areas of society and life. They can help us solve technical problems, research products, learn about interesting places or discover new recipes. Recent developments in North Africa demonstrate their ability to bring citizens together to express political power. Social media will play a key role in the discussion of important, future topics for Europe like a common energy strategy and foreign policy. However, certain groups are becoming detached from these developments. One can even speak of a broken link regarding communication cultures. This is an issue since bottom-up movements are highly relevant for politicians, marketing experts, and journalists who would like to know what customers or citizens think about initiatives, products, or publications. However, it is not possible to process manually the sheer amount of information generated in multiple languages on social networks. We need language technologies that are able to analyse these streams in real time.

Market Awareness and Customer Acceptance. Language technology is a key part of business and consumer software but often hidden inside other, more visible products. Customer acceptance of LT has recently been shown to be high. For example, market research by the Ford Motor Company indicates that their voice control system, Ford SYNC, is widely accepted [37]. 60% of Ford vehicle owners use voice commands in their cars. Non-Ford owners report a three-fold increase in their willingness to consider Ford models while 32% of existing customers admit that the technology played an important role in their purchase decision. Language technology has a tremendous market potential.

One Market, Many Languages. Support for the 23 official languages of the EU has major economic, social and political implications. Europe currently lags behind countries such as India (22 official languages) and South Africa (11 national languages). Government programmes in these two countries actively foster the development of language technology for a significant number of official languages [38, 39]. Mobile devices are an even more important bridge between humans and information technology. Google already provides free translation services in 3,306 different language pairs as well as voice input for 16 languages and speech output for 24 languages. Apple's App Store has demonstrated how premium content and products can be marketed for free and for a fee. Europe must address this global competition.

Secure Europe. The effective persecution of illegal online activities such as fraud and identity theft requires automatic tools that can help detect crimes and monitor offenders. Language technology can help to build systems that can monitor, analyse and summarise large amounts of text, audio and video data in different languages and from different sources.

This collection of solutions was influenced by bigger trends (see Chapter 3.1). Many of these products and services are only available online. For example, Facebook and Twitter enabled recent political developments in North Africa. In Europe, the idea of social innovation has recently sparked an interest as it "offers an effective approach to respond to social challenges by mobilising people's creativity to develop solutions and make a better use of scarce resources" [40]. Social innovation is part of Europe's 2020 strategy and critically relies on active involvement of citizens, which in turn calls for supportive multilingual language technologies.

Multilingualism has become the global norm rather than the exception [19]. Future applications that embed information and communication technology require sophisticated language technologies. Fully speech-enabled autonomous robots could help in disaster areas by rescuing travellers trapped in vehicles or by giving first aid. Language technology can significantly contribute towards improving social inclusion. Language technology can help us provide answers to urgent social challenges while creating genuine business opportunities. Language technology can now automate the very processes of translation, content production, and knowledge management for all European languages. It can also empower intuitive language/speech-based interfaces for household electronics, machinery, vehicles, computers and robots. In addition to these vertical societal challenges there are multiple horizontal properties that future language technologies need to exhibit. One of these properties is situation or context awareness. Many or even most applications sketched above need to exhibit a certain level of situation or context awareness. The challenge is to design and implement a paradigm in which language technologies are no longer static applications but able to adapt themselves to specific situations, trends and contexts such as, for example, user preferences or user interests. Security applications need to be aware of criminal or violent tendencies in communication patterns. E-participation systems need to be aware of interest in societal issues and need to have access to internet debates and the opinion of large online communities towards certain topics. Tools for the analysis of market awareness need methods for reputation mining, customer relationship systems need algorithms for attitude analysis.

2.4 MARKET OPPORTUNITIES

The market offers tremendous business potential for European language technology companies, especially for online retailers, language services, LT usage in key markets, data intensive scenarios and selected devices and environments. (This section is partially based on [41]).

Most online retailers are limited to small segments, the largest of which scarcely exceeds 60 million in population [42]: 82% of European retailers operate in only a single language, 11% in only two, and only 2% provide services in five or more languages; only 21% of European retailers support cross-border transactions. Although 51% of European retailers sell via the internet, a vanishing small number of Europeans currently engage in online cross-border purchases. Language technology that lowers the burden and costs of translation and localisation for European languages would not only open the European market to European businesses, but enable them to access the estimated population of one billion individuals worldwide who speak one of Europe's major languages, with accompanying economic benefit for European companies. The market for LT software is currently expected to grow to 30 billion Euros by 2015 (versus 20 billion Euros today). European enterprises – particularly the more than 500 active European SMEs – have the potential to dominate the field if they can offer compelling solutions to Europe's needs for online businesses and other fields.

Aside from the sales potential for online retailers, deployment of LT would increase overall demand for language-related services, currently worth ca. 5 billion Euros in Europe (expected to grow to ca. 8 billion Euros by 2015). As translation becomes the norm rather than the exception, the translation market, one which Europe currently dominates, would be expected to see substantially faster growth than anticipated.

In addition, dedicated LT-intense services will gain importance. Examples are technical translation supported by LT in the automotive domain, automatic interpreting for tourism and culture, or speaker verification for financial services and banking. The European LT industry is in a good position to serve these markets, since European LT companies specialise in these domains.

The business role of LT can be characterised in terms of its relation to the Big Data market (estimated at ca. 4 billion Euros in 2012, expected to grow to ca. 13 billion Euros by 2015), cloud-based models for distribution and computation (expected to reach 45 billion Euros in the near future) or business data intelligence gathering and analysis (currently a 27 billion Euros market). In all these areas LT will be crucial for assuring high quality and meaningful use of data and data infrastructures.

Finally, certain types of systems and devices will require LT for core functionality. Mobile devices currently drive 43% of current IT growth; embedded systems are currently an 800 billion Euros p. a. industry. At the moment U.S.-based companies have a lead in these areas, but their offerings often do not consider multilingualism as a base requirement. This will create a market opportunity in the billions of euros for European LT companies.

MAJOR TRENDS IN INFORMATION AND COMMUNICATION TECHNOLOGIES

3.1 THE CURRENT STATE

Networked computers are ubiquitous. They come in different shapes and forms (desktop, laptop, mobile phones, tablets, ebook readers, etc.) or are embedded in devices, objects, and systems such as, for example, cameras, washing machines, televisions, cars, heating systems, robots, traffic control systems. Software is usually available in multiple human languages. Global standardisation efforts such as Unicode solved the problem of representing and displaying different alphabets and special characters. Mobile devices and social media are reshaping how and when we communicate with one another using the tools and devices we use both in business and private life. The way we interact with computers is no longer restricted to graphical interfaces and keyboards, but it is being extended through touch screens, voice interfaces and dialogue systems, and mobile devices with accelerometers that tell the device how it is held by the user.

Language technology is currently not well integrated into applications and interfaces – to the end user, spelling, grammar checking and maybe search seem to be the only notable exceptions. Apple's introduction of the mobile assistant Siri on the iPhone and a similar product by Google illustrate the trend towards more intelligent language-based interaction.

The web represents much of our knowledge. It emerged as a collection of static documents. Nowadays it is first and foremost a collection of systems and databases that can be queried through APIs, and applications such as Google Mail, Facebook, eBay and Amazon. Many people only need one application on their computers: a web browser. Others use netbooks whose operating system more or less *is* the browser (Chromium OS). Behind the scenes, there is already a considerable amount of language technology incorporated in web applications such as search engines, dialogue systems, or machine translation services but these are not immediately visible or recognisable by the user as language technologies as such.

3.2 HARDWARE AND SOFTWARE

Networked computers come in many shapes and forms, from mobile phones to tablets, netbooks, ultra-portable laptops, small desktop computers and ebook readers to devices such as radios, televisions, gaming consoles and other entertainment devices with built-in wireless and access to, for example, RSS feeds, internet radio stations or youtube, cameras or house-hold appliances such as fridges, coffee machines or scales that push the user's weight to the cloud from where it can be monitored using an app on the smartphone. The next hardware revolution will be wearable computers. Google has already demonstrated a prototype of their Google Glasses product in which the computer visuals are projected into a head-up display. This approach can be used to provide the user with a true augmented reality perspective and a hands-free computing environment which immediately brings

G. Rehm and H. Uszkoreit (eds.), *META-NET Strategic Research Agenda for Multilingual Europe 2020,* White Paper Series, DOI: 10.1007/978-3-642-36349-8_3, © The Author(s) 2013

up the question how to interact with this device – by using only your voice?

The shape and size of computers is no longer determined by the shape and size of their internal hardware components. Due to breakthroughs in miniaturisation, their form now truly follows their function. While computers and devices with embedded systems get smaller and smaller, the distributed data centres around the world get bigger and bigger – both in terms of number and size. The concept of cloud computing and storing data in dedicated data centres from where the data can be accessed by multiple devices, is already mainstream and used by millions of consumers world-wide. An important reason for the cloud's success is the fact that, by now, people tend to have more than one computer. A not too unusual setup may include a laptop, a smartphone, a tablet and another computer as a dedicated media centre. Cloud services are ideal for synchronising data between many devices.

The trends in the software area are much more multi-dimensional. Here we can only scratch the surface and highlight several recent developments and current trends.

Communication: A cornerstone of today's computer use is communication, be it more direct communication via traditional e-mail, instant messaging, text-based chat systems, video chat between two people or larger groups or indirect communication and staying in touch with friends, acquaintances and colleagues via social networks such as Twitter, Facebook, LinkedIn, Instagram or social media such as blogs, YouTube, or Pinterest. Millions of people world-wide are always online using several different networked devices including their phones.

Search and Information Services: An important use case of any type of device is to search for information and to make use of information services. Important applications are web search engines, online encyclopedias, news sites, digital libraries such as Europeana, meta-search engines and RSS feed aggregators etc.

Location-based Services: Search queries are often coupled to the user's location. Location-based services enable the user to search for information in his or her geographic area, to make use of online maps, navigation systems, recommender systems or to find tweets or photos from the neighbourhood.

Media monitoring: Search and retrieval enable users to find information they already know about or suspect exist. Both are about finding the needles in the haystack. Media monitoring and applications with a certain level of situation awareness are not about finding documents or items, they are about keeping track of the state of the world. Applications for this purpose are coming to the market at a rapid pace.

E-Commerce and Shopping: World-wide billions of Euros are spent each year using general online shops such as Amazon or eBay or shops run by specific brands or services, reservation and booking, online banking and brokering services etc.

Media and Entertainment: Different types of media (photos, videos, music, sounds, text and multimedia documents, audio and video podcasts, ebooks, films, tv programmes etc.) play an important role. Not only personal media such as photos or videos and other user-generated content are often posted to social networks, songs, photos or videos created by third parties are also often shared using social networks. Almost all of the media mentioned above can be purchased in online stores, for consumption on any device. Another important software category is games, from online Flash games to games that are embedded into social networks, location-based games, multi-player games with millions of users to very simple but also very successful casual games such as Angry Birds.

App and Media Stores: The success of ecommerce platforms [17], online shopping and the increased use of digital media led to app and media stores. By now it is possible to buy or rent almost every movie ever made, to buy music, to stream music from the cloud onto your device and to buy software and mobile apps through dedicated stores without any need to ship physical media. An important development is in-app purchasing, especially on mobile devices: with a single tap of a finger it is possible to buy, within a specific app, additional modules, components or data sets for a small price.

Personal Information Management: With the ever increasing number of personal and professional contacts (including social networks), meetings and personal errands to run, there is a big trend towards personal information management. This includes address and contacts databases that are often integrated into larger applications such as Google Contacts (embedded in, among others, Google Mail) or Apple's AddressBook (used in Apple Mail). Cloud-integration is an important feature, so that contact information (including names, email addresses, phone numbers, photos etc.), calendar entries and "to do" items are always available on all devices.

Office Applications: The classic office applications – word processors, spreadsheets, presentations – are still important in the professional context and also in home use. Nowadays, there are several applications to choose from including open source software, cloud-based services and applications for Apple's iOS. Almost all office suites use the cloud to enable the user to, for example, finish work on a presentation at the desktop computer where the document is automatically pushed to the cloud and to continue working on the presentation on a mobile device on the way home.

One of the most basic common denominators of all pieces of software is language which plays a central and integral part in practically every single tool or application. However, language technology as such (including text analysis, information retrieval and extraction, spelling and grammar checking, speech recognition and synthesis, dialogue systems etc.) is usually completely hidden, integrated into bigger applications, working behind the scenes. There is, however, a clear trend to embed

language technologies not only at the level of the single application but on the level of the operating system. Another important factor of current computing is communicating and interacting with other people or groups of people, both on the personal level and also for business purposes. A third crucial ingredient of computing today is information, especially structured information which is annotated based on specific standards (see, for example, the family of standards around XML, Semantic Web, Linked Open Data, Web Services, Big Data etc.).

3.3 CURRENT TRENDS AND MEGA-TRENDS

In the following we sketch some of the current trends and mega-trends, grouped into three sections.

Internet: The internet will continue to be *the* main driving force behind future developments in information and communication technologies. There are several mega-trends tightly coupled to the internet and network technologies: among these are cloud computing and cloud services, including cloud storage, as well as linked open data and the semantic web. Social media and social networks will continue to change everything and to penetrate the market further, including niche markets, driven by location-based services. With the predominance of social networks we expect a certain convergence of digital identities that will enable users to have and to maintain one central digital identity that feeds into their multiple social network profiles. Exchanging and distributing personal data and information (photos, videos, music etc.) in a secure way will become easier. We further expect more broad deployment and general acceptance of services in the areas of e-democracy and e-government (including open data portals) and a continued increase of e-commerce platforms [17] and services. A perceived general information overload will continue to be a problem, although modern search engines, aggregation services and user interfaces help a lot. New business models and ways to distribute content or services to the end-user will continue to emerge (see the different app stores and approaches such as in-app purchases).

People: Information and communication technologies are used by people – the predominance of social networks and being always-on using smartphones, tablets and laptops, is responsible for the fact that the way people interact, communicate and do business with one another will continue to be redefined and reshaped completely, including novel approaches for participation and public deliberation processes. Communication tools such as email, twitter, facebook etc. are mainstream by now and used across all age groups. This trend will continue. The trend to use social networks and location-based services to find "faces and places", items or places of interest or new acquaintances with similar hobbies will continue (along with a more in-depth discussion of privacy issues). We expect a tighter connection between the data stored in social networks as well as tools for personal information management and the linked open data cloud.

Hardware and Software: Many internet companies operate under the slogan "mobile first". Accessing the web on mobile devices will overtake the use of desktops and laptops very soon. There is also a tendency for completely novel mobile devices with Apple's iPad and Google's Glasses being two prime examples. More and more household-appliances get connected to the internet (tv, radio, gaming consoles, refrigerator, scales, coffee machine, lamps etc.), ultimately leading to the Internet of Things. Many of these devices will not have displays but voice-driven interfaces. We expect a seamless integration of mobile devices into the hardware landscape at home including simplified data and application transfer and exchange among arbitrary mobile or stationary devices, playing music or movies on displays or video projectors etc. Very soon there will not be a need anymore for the average user to own a laptop or desktop com-

puter because mobile devices will cover all basic needs. The capacity and bandwidth of networks will continue to grow, mobile telecommunication networks will gradually become more important than, for example, ADSL lines. The quality of voice or video calls will continue to improve, phones and all other devices will continue to become faster, have more storage as well as 3D-capable displays that offer more intricate modes of interaction. Mobile phones will have built-in facilities to replace credit cards for payment purposes, effectively replacing the wallet. Finally, the market for apps, especially mobile apps, will continue to grow. Nowadays many companies, services and events have their own app that users can interact with and that usually offer added value when compared to the respective website. Usability will continue to be a decisive factor: only those apps will be successful that users can interact with intuitively right away.

Information and communication technologies will continue to be ubiquitous, available wherever and whenever needed. They will combine widely distributed applications, resources and data and will be able to adapt to the location, situation and needs of the user including current emotions, habits and goals. As can be seen by the success of Wikipedia and other collaboratively edited knowledge bases, it is only a matter of time until one or more gigantic digital models of our world will exist that consist of interlinked and overlapping components. Naturally, languages and especially the automatic processing of languages using language technologies will play a key role in this development. Now is the time to realise the needed breakthroughs. High performance, robust machine translation and related language technology services are urgently needed. There is a huge window of opportunity for consumer-oriented language technology.

Large global platforms for end-user-services have become the predominant innovation drivers for language technology solutions. Well known examples are web services such as Google Search, now integrating the new Knowledge Graph concept network, speech-enabled search [43], web translation services, social networks such as Twitter and Facebook, and combinations of hardware and operating systems such as iOS or Android. The trend towards widely used platforms will drastically facilitate the spreading of innovative language technologies. LT has a good chance of becoming *the* essential feature for the success of the next generation of platforms and services. At closer inspection, the integration of LT in current platforms is very limited, scratching only the surface of what will be possible in the near future.

3.4 SELECTED TREND: BIG DATA, LINKED OPEN DATA AND THE DATA CHALLENGE

There are two important trends concerning data on the web. First, the web is becoming translingual, with content and knowledge being accessible across languages, allowing users to search for and interact with knowledge, but also with devices which are part of the Web of Things, accessible for everybody in their own language. Second, more and more amounts of data – *Big Data* – are being made available online. Big data leads to new challenges in terms of scalability, but also to many new innovations and application scenarios.

The Translingual Web will enable world wide, borderless communication and commerce. Linked Open Data based on the Semantic Web will be able to support language technologies for improved quality, e. g., in machine translation or cross-lingual search. On the other hand, language technology can support Linked Open Data. It provides the means to create inter- and intra language links and relations to textual knowledge.

Our three priority themes (see Chapter 6) are related to the Translingual Web and data. The Translingual Cloud will benefit from data available across languages. Translation technologies will also help to address data challenges,

like building and cleaning data sets that span across languages or providing links between data sets within one or between languages. Multilingual access is an important requirement for a European vision of e-government and e-participation services. On the one hand, language technology can make use of open, governmental data that is made available on portals such as data.gov.uk or within the upcoming European data portal. On the other hand, improving language technologies is inevitable for realising multilingual access to public sector data for all European citizens, as recommended by the European Interoperability Framework for European public services [44]: the sheer amount of data and language barriers between data sets are obstacles that can only be removed with language technologies (e. g., machine translation, cross-lingual information access and information extraction). Finally, one application scenario of Socially-Aware Interactive Assistants are multilingual virtual meetings that make use of shared data sets that provide information about individuals, organisations and interaction settings.

In order to be able to overcome language barriers, data infrastructures need to be made available, while carefully taking licensing and data provenance into account. Existing language and localisation resources (e. g., terminological, lexical data or translation memories) need to be transformed into linked open data. Only then will they be able to play a key role for creating truly multilingual linked open data. Standardisation is crucial when it comes to implementing the infrastructure. So are reference implementations that deal with standardised data and metadata for human language in LT, localisation, CMS, CAT and TMS tools, to assure that standards can be put into action easily and get wide adoption.

Language Technology will also play a key role for Big Data (Figure 4). Building future-proof solutions for big data analysis is impossible without Language Technology. Big data analysis will not be slightly better if we include language technology – it simply will not happen. We cannot download big data into a database and then build applications on top of it – we will need to process it sensibly and that sense will need to be based on language. This challenge not only relates to structured big data but also to any type of unstructured data including text documents and social media streams, esentially any sequential symbolic process of meaningful information. LT will build bridges from big data to knowledge, from unstructured data to structured data, and can finally lead to what some people are already referring to as Big Semantics. Language Technology will become the foundation for organising, analysing and extracting data in a truly useful way.

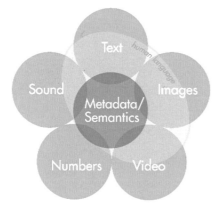

4: Human language in the world of data

To achieve success in these trends, various prerequisites need to be fulfilled. Linked open data sets need to be enriched with multilingual information. For textual knowledge we can expect that the enrichment will trigger a bootstrapping process. Here, bootstrapping means that existing Semantic Web vocabularies and data sets will be enriched with multilingual information in a first step. They can then be exploited as background knowledge for improved text analysis. Afterwards they can be fed back into the world of linked open data. Models such as, e. g., Lemon for enriching ontologies with multilingual, linguistic information will lead to richer resources and quality in the areas of machine translation, question answering, information extraction or textual entailment. This will create a synergetic cycle, in which the Semantic Web

and deep text analysis benefit from each other, effectively bootstrapping the Translingual Web. For realising these synergies, methodologies need to be developed both for high quality, manually created linked open data resources and for big data, e. g., analysing activities of billions of users on the global, multilingual social web.

Another pre-requisite for the convergence of data and LT is the availability of free, open and interoperable data sources. Existing resources such as Wikipedia, DBpedia, Wikidata, Yago and OpenStreetMap need to be consolidated, based on standardised vocabularies to support interoperability and re-use. Core ontology vocabularies need to be translated into different languages. We need tools for cleaning up data, as well as mechanisms that can aggregate, summarise and repurpose content. For all LT applications that interact with data, the regulation of intellectual property rights is a problem that needs to be resolved soon. The web is a global space, and Europe has to find a legal approach that supports both local R&D while fostering global competitiveness.

In FP7, projects and efforts such as DBpedia, Monnet, Wikidata and META-NET's META-SHARE have started tackling some of the problems discussed above. Organisations like ISO TC37 SC4, GALA and the World Wide Web Consortium support this work by providing standardised building blocks for application development and data sharing. Europe is in a good position to be in the driver's seat of the data challenge, both for human knowledge and big data, effectively creating multiple new data value chains (Figure 5).

3.5 SELECTED TREND: FROM CLOUD COMPUTING TO SKY COMPUTING

A major megatrend is known as cloud computing. A large proportion of IT solutions is already offered through the internet, forecasts predict that it will increase rapidly.

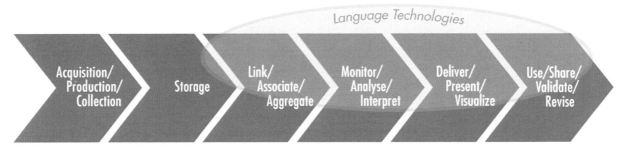

5: Language technology in the Data Value Chain

Computing may be offered on different levels of abstraction ranging from Infrastructures as a Service (IaaS) via Platforms as a Service (PaaS) to the powerful concept of providing any suitable software product as an internet service (Software as a Service, SaaS). Especially the latter concept has far-reaching, mainly beneficial, implications for distribution, support, customisation, maintenance and pricing. It also opens new opportunities for software evolution by emerging dynamic schemes of integration, evaluation, adaptation and scaling. A well-known example are the Google Docs office applications. In language technology an increasing number of solutions are already offered as free or commercial web services, among them machine translation, language checking and text-to-speech conversion.

A special challenge for cloud computing is the need for trust. Since the services are rendered outside their sphere of control, customers demand sufficient safeguards securing performance, data protection, and persistence. Large European users of translation technology do not send their corporate language data to the existing large online translation services because the service providers do not offer a trust mechanisms. The situation is even more severe for business intelligence applications where the confidentiality of the collected information can be mission critical for planning and decision processes.

The most far-reaching development is the sky computing paradigm. Although the cloud metaphor originated from the widely used graphical icon for the internet symbolis-

ing the entire global network outside the user's computer, soon the term became applied to any computing service provided on the internet. The term sky computing extends the notion of cloud computing. It was coined for a setup in which clouds are combined into complex services, environments with workflows realising functionalities that exceed the capabilities of the individual services. Language technologies are prime candidates for sky computing setups since they are often a component of complex applications such as services supporting knowledge discovery, business intelligence or text production. Taking into account the large number of languages, language variants and subject domains, a sky computing setup can provide a much larger number of language and task-specific workflows through service composition than a traditional software product. Small and medium technology enterprises will be able much more easily to enter the market, stay on the market and improve their services without having to cast all demanded service combinations into their product family or into a range of bilateral OEM partnerships.

3.6 THE FUTURE ROLE OF LANGUAGE TECHNOLOGY

In the next years language technology will play a major and decisive role, as explained and demonstrated by the discussion of megatrends and selected trends above.

The IT research and advisory company Gartner publishes the "Gartner Hype Cycle" every year. These studies are meant to provide strategists and planners with an assessment of the maturity, business benefit and future direction of more than 1,900 technologies, grouped into 92 areas [45]. Among the ones most prominently featured by the report are big data, 3D printing, activity streams, Internet TV, Near Field Communication (NFC) payment, cloud computing and media tablets. The Gartner analysts also mention several significant scenarios, that appear to be extremely promising on multiple levels but for which more enabling technologies are needed before they can be put into practice. Among them are "smarter things" and, most notably, "the human way to interact with technology". In fact, if we take a closer look at the 2012 hype cycle, reproduced in Figure 6, we notice that a total of 13 of the 48 technologies listed are language technologies, many of which are in the early "technology trigger" phase. Among the top emerging and key enabling technologies

of 2012 and the coming years are, to list only a few, Automatic Content Recognition, Natural-Language Question Answering, Speech-to-Speech Translation, Complex Event-Processing, Social Analytics, Text Analytics and Speech Recognition. This assessment clearly shows that now is the time to invest in strategic research in the area of language technology and to go for a major, continent-wide push. One thing is certain: these technologies *will* come – they will be responsible for the biggest revolution in IT since the introduction of the graphical user interface and they will generate many jobs and countless business as well as social opportunities. Europe can now decide if it wants to play only a minor role, following the US and Asia, or it wants to move ahead and take the lead itself.

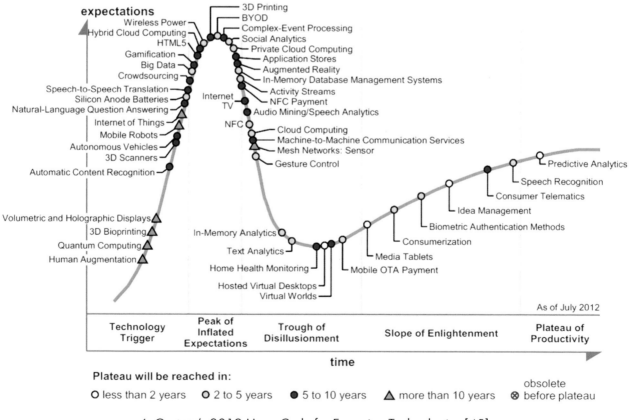

6: Gartner's 2012 Hype Cycle for Emerging Technologies [45]

LANGUAGE TECHNOLOGY 2012: CURRENT STATE AND OPPORTUNITIES

4.1 CURRENT STATE OF EUROPEAN LANGUAGE TECHNOLOGY

Answering the question on the current state of a whole R&D field is both difficult and complex. For language technology, even though partial answers exist in terms of business figures, scientific challenges and results from educational studies, nobody has collected these indicators and provided comparable reports for a substantial number of European languages yet. In order to arrive at a comprehensive answer, META-NET prepared the White Paper Series "Europe's Languages in the Digital Age" that describes the current state of language technology support for 30 European languages [12]. This immense undertaking has been in preparation since mid 2010 and was published in the Summer of 2012. More than 200 experts from academia and industry participated to the 30 volumes as co-authors and contributors. White Papers were written for the following 30 European languages (including all 23 official EU languages): Basque, Bulgarian, Catalan, Croatian, Czech, Danish, Dutch, English, Estonian, Finnish, French, Galician, German, Greek, Hungarian, Icelandic, Irish, Italian, Latvian, Lithuanian, Maltese, Norwegian, Polish, Portuguese, Romanian, Serbian, Slovak, Slovene, Spanish, Swedish.

The current state of support through language technology varies considerably from one language community to another. In order to compare the situation between languages, the META-NET White Paper Series introduces an evaluation based on two sample application areas (Machine Translation and Speech Processing) and one underlying technology (Text Analytics) as well as basic Language Resources needed for building LT applications (for example, very large collections of texts for machine learning purposes). For each language, support through language technology was categorised using a five-point scale (1. excellent support; 2. good support; 3. moderate support; 4. fragmentary support; 5. weak or no support) and measured according to the following key criteria:

Machine Translation: quality of existing technologies, number of language pairs covered, coverage of linguistic phenomena and domains, quality and size of parallel corpora, amount and variety of applications.

Speech Processing: quality of existing speech recognition and synthesis technologies, coverage of domains, number and size of existing corpora, amount and variety of available applications.

Text Analytics: quality and coverage of existing technologies (morphology, syntax, semantics), coverage of linguistic phenomena and domains, amount and variety of available applications, quality and size of (annotated) corpora, quality and coverage of lexical resources (e. g., WordNet) and grammars.

Resources: quality/size of text, speech and parallel corpora, quality/coverage of lexical resources and grammars.

The more than 200 co-authors of and contributors to the White Papers prepared initial language-specific as-

G. Rehm and H. Uszkoreit (eds.), *META-NET Strategic Research Agenda for Multilingual Europe 2020*, White Paper Series, DOI: 10.1007/978-3-642-36349-8_4, © The Author(s) 2013

sessments of technology support by assessing ca. 25 different applications, tools and resources along seven different axes and criteria. Later on, the 30 individual and language-specific matrices were condensed in order to arrive at a single score per language and area.

Figure 7 demonstrates that the differences in technology support between the various languages and areas are dramatic and alarming. In all four areas, English is ahead of the other languages but even support for English is far from being perfect. While there are good quality software and resources available for a few larger languages and application areas, others, usually smaller or very small languages, have substantial gaps. Many languages lack even basic technologies for text analytics and essential language resources. Others have basic resources but the implementation of, for example, semantic methods is still far away. Therefore, a large-scale effort is needed to attain the ambitious goal of providing high-quality language technologies for all European languages.

The White Paper Series contains assessments for each of the 30 languages. Currently no language, not even English, has the technological support it deserves. Also, the number of badly supported and under-resourced languages is unacceptable if we do not want to give up the principles of solidarity and subsidiarity in Europe.

4.2 THE DANGER OF DIGITAL LANGUAGE EXTINCTION

On the occasion of the European Day of Languages 2012, September 26, we announced the results of our "Europe's Languages in the Digital Age" study to the public through a press release translated into 30 languages. The headline was: *At Least 21 European Languages in Danger of Digital Extinction – Good News and Bad News on the European Day of Languages.*

We were overwhelmed by the immediate, very big interest in the topic and our findings. The first articles appeared online only hours after we sent out the first press releases. We also received many requests for radio and television interviews. Journalists called to collect additional statements and to enquire about specific details.

By now we estimate ca. 550 mentions in the online press in Europe and also multiple mentions in the international press (from Mexico to New Zealand). We also estimate that our press release generated more than 75 mentions in traditional newspapers. Representatives of META-NET took part in about 45 radio interviews (for example, in Germany, Greece, Iceland, Ireland, Latvia, Norway). We estimate that an additional 25 radio and more than 25 television programmes (including coverage in, for example, Iceland and Latvia) reported on our findings.

A few significant newspapers and blogs that reported on the study: Der Standard (Austria); Politiken (Denmark); Tiede (Finland); Heise Newsticker, Süddeutsche Zeitung (Germany); Πρώτο Θέμα, Καθημερινή (Greece); Fréttablaðið (Iceland); Wired (Italy); Delo, Dnevnik (Slovenia); El Mundo (Spain); Huffington Post (UK); Mashable, NBC News, Reddit (USA), see http://www.meta-net.eu/whitepapers/press-coverage.

The echo generated by our press release shows that Europe is very passionate about its languages, concerned about digital language extinction and that it is also very interested in the idea of establishing a solid language technology base for overcoming language barriers.

4.3 EDUCATION AND TRAINING

An indispensable prerequisite for innovative research and technology development are highly qualified researchers and software developers. In the ca. two years it took us to prepare this agenda, we talked to many companies. With almost no exceptions the industry representatives mentioned the lack of qualified personnel to be a significant problem for their further growth and diminish-

	Support: excellent	good	moderate	fragmentary	weak/none
Machine Translation		English	French, Spanish	Catalan, Dutch, German, Hungarian, Italian, Polish, Romanian	Basque, Bulgarian, Croatian, Czech, Danish, Estonian, Finnish, Galician, Greek, Icelandic, Irish, Latvian, Lithuanian, Maltese, Norwegian, Portuguese, Serbian, Slovak, Slovene, Swedish
Speech		English	Czech, Dutch, Finnish, French, German, Italian, Portuguese, Spanish	Basque, Bulgarian, Catalan, Danish, Estonian, Galician, Greek, Hungarian, Irish, Norwegian, Polish, Serbian, Slovak, Slovene, Swedish	Croatian, Icelandic, Latvian, Lithuanian, Maltese, Romanian
Text Analytics		English	Dutch, French, German, Italian, Spanish	Basque, Bulgarian, Catalan, Czech, Danish, Finnish, Galician, Greek, Hungarian, Norwegian, Polish, Portuguese, Romanian, Slovak, Slovene, Swedish	Croatian, Estonian, Icelandic, Irish, Latvian, Lithuanian, Maltese, Serbian
Language Resources		English	Czech, Dutch, French, German, Hungarian, Italian, Polish, Spanish, Swedish	Basque, Bulgarian, Catalan, Croatian, Danish, Estonian, Finnish, Galician, Greek, Norwegian, Portuguese, Romanian, Serbian, Slovak, Slovene	Icelandic, Irish, Latvian, Lithuanian, Maltese

7: State of language technology support for 30 European languages in four different areas

ing factor for producing innovative technologies. Europe's academic programmes in Natural Language Processing, Computational Linguistics, Language Technologies etc. need to be further strengthened and advertised on an international level and made more attractive for potential students. In a later implementation phase of this agenda we plan to introduce coordinated training programmes for IT professionals and software developers who are not yet familiar with LT so that they are made aware of our tools, resources and technologies and learn how to make use of them in their own IT landscapes. The lack of skilled personnel currently is a, if not *the* major bottleneck for many small and medium companies and also research centres.

4.4 CHALLENGES AND CHANCES

The first language applications such as voice-based user interfaces and dialogue systems were developed for highly specialised domains and purposes, and often exhibited rather limited performance. By now, however, there are huge market opportunities in the communication, collaboration, education and entertainment industries for integrating language technologies into general information and communication technologies, games, cultural heritage sites, edutainment packages, libraries, simulation environments and training programmes. Mobile information services, computer-assisted language learning software, e-learning environments, self-assessment tools and plagiarism detection software are just a few application areas in which language technology can and will play an important role in the years to come. The success of social networks such as Twitter and Facebook demonstrates a further need for sophisticated language technologies that can monitor posts, summarise discussions, suggest opinion trends, detect emotional responses, identify copyright infringements or track misuse.

Language technology represents a tremendous opportunity for the European Union. It can help address the complex issue of multilingualism in Europe. Citizens need to communicate across language borders, criss-crossing the European common market – language technology can help overcome this final barrier while supporting the free and open use of individual languages. Looking even a bit further into the future, innovative European multilingual language technology could provide a benchmark for other multilingual communities in the world [19, 20, 21]. This, in turn, would generate additional market opportunities for European companies.

The automated translation and speech processing tools currently available fall short of the envisaged goals. The dominant actors in the field are primarily companies based in the US. As early as the late 1970s, the EU realised the profound relevance of LT as a driver of European unity, and began funding its first research projects. At the same time, national projects were set up that generated valuable results, but never led to a concerted European effort. In contrast to these highly selective funding efforts, other multilingual societies such as India (22 official languages) and South Africa (11 official languages) have recently set up long-term national programmes for language research and technology development.

Today the predominant actors in language technology rely on statistical approaches, but rule-based approaches reach comparable performance in a different way. Not surprisingly, cross-fertilisation between these approaches has been sought and reached already. Both in combination and in separation there are promising ideas to advance these approaches. On the one hand, analysing the deeper structural properties of languages in terms of syntax and semantics as well as making use of different types of knowledge and inferencing is a promising way forward if we want to build applications that perform well across the entire range of European languages. On the other hand, we need statistical models that go beyond the current ones and extract more dependencies from the data. They can be related to existing linguistic theories, but they might also be very much different. The dependencies have to be deeply integrated and require research on statistical decision theory and machine learning along with efficient algorithms and implementations.

The European Union is funding projects such as EuroMatrix and EuroMatrix+ (since 2006) and iTranslate4 (since 2010), that carry out basic and applied research and also generate resources for establishing high quality language technology solutions for several European languages. European research in the area of language technology has already achieved a number of outstanding successes. For example, the translation services of the EU now use the Moses open source machine translation software, which has been mainly developed in European research projects [46]. In addition, national funding used to have huge impact. For example, the Verbmobil project, funded by the German Ministry of Education and Research (BMBF) between 1993 and 2000, pushed Germany to the top position in the world in terms of speech translation research for a time. Rather than building on the important results and success stories generated by these projects, Europe has tended to pursue isolated research activities with a less pervasive impact on the market. The economic value of even the earliest efforts can be seen in the number of spin-offs: a company such as Trados, founded back in 1984, was sold to the UK-based SDL in 2005.

Today's hybrid language technology mixing deep processing with statistical methods will be able to bridge the gap between all European languages and beyond. But there is a dramatic difference between Europe's languages in terms of both the maturity of the research and the state of readiness with respect to language technology solutions. Three key ingredients are needed to realise the technology visions described in Chapter 5: the right actors, a strategic programme and appropriate support. Until 2010 the European language industries had to be considered highly fragmented at best. They consist of hundreds of innovative and ambitious small and medium enter-

prises, language technologists and language professionals. Several thousand private companies provide technologically supported language services such as translation, authoring/editing and language training.

In 2010 META-NET (see Appendix D, p. 83) has started to bring the fragmented community together and to assemble researchers from the different subfields and also related scientific fields (humanities, psychology, social sciences etc.), universities, research centres, language communities, national language institutions, smaller and medium companies as well as large enterprises, officials, administrators, politicians under one roof: META (Multilingual Europe Technology Alliance). By now META has more than 650 members in more than 50 countries. META-NET's vision and planning process has involved more than 300 companies, of which more than 200 have already joined META. During this process, a number of language technology providers decided to form the first LT business association that recently transformed into the organisation LT-Innovate. The new association involving more than one hundred SMEs is currently working on proposals for improving the mechanisms and support of innovation processes in our field. These proposals could become an important contribution to META's future planning work, especially in the specification and dynamic adaptation of the META-NET roadmaps.

Now that the European LT community has been brought together we can present our vision and strategic research agenda. The whole META community has helped to shape this agenda (see Appendices B and C, p. 78 ff., for more details). META-NET hopes to raise enough awareness, enthusiasm and, eventually, support to develop and, finally, to bring about a truly multilingual Europe based on sophisticated language technologies. We suggest to set up a shared programme with the goal of concentrating our research efforts on three priority research themes (Chapter 6).

LANGUAGE TECHNOLOGY 2020: THE META-NET TECHNOLOGY VISION

5.1 THE NEXT IT REVOLUTION

People communicate using the languages they have known since early childhood, yet computers remained ignorant of their users' languages for a long time. It took many years until they could reliably handle scripts of languages other than English. It took even longer until computers could check the spelling of texts and read them aloud for the visually impaired.

On the web we can now get rough translations and search for texts containing a word, even if the word occurs in a different form from the one we search for. But when it comes to interpreting certain input and responding correctly, computers only "understand" simple artificial languages such as Java, C++ and HTML.

In the next IT revolution computers will master our languages. Just as they already understand measurements and formats for dates and times, the operating systems of tomorrow will know human languages. They may not reach the linguistic performance of educated people and they will not yet know enough about the world to understand everything, but they will be much more useful than they are today and will further enhance our work and life.

5.2 COMMUNICATION AMONG PEOPLE

Language is our most natural medium for interpersonal communication, but computers cannot yet help much with regular conversation. With thousands of languages spoken on our planet, however, we will find ourselves in situations where language breaks down. In such situations we must rely on technology to help bridge the gap. While current translation technologies have been successfully demonstrated for limited numbers of languages and themes, computers have not yet fulfilled the dream of automatic translation. By the year 2020, however, with sufficient research effort on high-quality automatic translation and robust accurate speech recognition, reliable dialogue translation for face-to-face conversation and telecommunication will be possible for at least hundreds of languages, across multiple subject fields and text types, both spoken and written.

Today we use computers for producing and reading texts (emails, instant messages, novels, technical documents etc.), checking spelling and grammar, and finding alternatives for words. Enterprises already use LT products for checking conformance to corporate terminology and style guidelines. In 2020 authoring software will also check for appropriate style according to genre and purpose and help evaluate comprehensibility. It will flag potential errors, suggest corrections, and use authoring memories to proactively suggest completions of started sentences or even whole paragraphs.

Google Translate and other translation services provide access to information and knowledge for hundreds of millions of users across language boundaries. This technology is important for personal use and for numerous professional applications, e. g., intelligence jobs in which analysts search large bodies of text for relevant information.

G. Rehm and H. Uszkoreit (eds.), *META-NET Strategic Research Agenda for Multilingual Europe 2020,*
White Paper Series, DOI: 10.1007/978-3-642-36349-8_5, © The Author(s) 2013

The European Commission uses similar translation technology provided by European research projects, but the translations produced by these technologies can only be used internally due to poor quality. Despite tremendous progress, it cannot yet help with the skyrocketing costs of outbound translation. Many translation services have started using machine translation, but further economic breakthroughs through increased translation quality are still ahead of us and will come in stages over the next ten years as the existing barriers for quality are overcome by new technologies that get closer to the structure and meaning behind human language.

For example, by 2020 tele-meetings utilising large displays and comfortable technology will be the norm for professional meetings. LT will be able to record, transcribe, and summarise meetings. Brainstorming will be facilitated by semantic lookup and structured display of relevant data, proposals, charts, pictures, and maps. This technology will simultaneously translate (interpret) the contributions of participants into as many languages as needed, and incrementally drafted summaries will be used for displaying the state of the discussion, including intermediate results and open issues. The software will be guided by partial understanding of the contents, i.e., by its semantic association with concepts in semantic models of domains and processes.

Language technology will have a major role in helping with the ever-growing volume of correspondence. Automatic authoring techniques will actively help users draft messages. Many organisations already employ e-mail response management software to filter, sort, and route incoming email and to suggest replies for recognised types of requests. By 2020, business email will be embedded in semantically structured process models to automate standardised communication. Even before 2020, email communication will be semantically analysed, checked for sentiment indicators, and summarised in reports. LT will also help to integrate content across all communication channels: telecommunication, meetings, email and chat, etc. Semantic integration into work processes, threading, and response management will be applied across channels, as will machine translation and analytics.

The rise of Web 2.0 (social networks and user-generated content) has confronted LT with a new set of challenges. Every user can become a content producer and large numbers of people can participate in communications. Some of these multi-directional mass communications have turned into effective instruments to solicit support, put pressure on leaders and decisions makers, create ideas, and find solutions. Communities can emerge in a matter of hours or days around admired works of art, shared preferences, or social issues. Citizen action movements, international NGOs, self-help groups, expert circles, and communities of concerned consumers can all organise using these technologies.

The social web cannot reach its potential because the large volumes of user-generated content quickly become unmanageable and difficult to understand. Participants, outside stakeholders, and concerned decision makers find it difficult to stay on top of new developments. Much of the often-cited wisdom of the crowds and their motivation and efforts are wasted because of information overload. With focused research efforts leading up to 2020, LT will be able to harness this deluge to monitor, analyse, summarise, structure, document, and visualise social media dynamics. Democracy and markets will be enriched by powerful new mechanisms for developing improved collective solutions and decisions.

Language technology can also help by converting language between different modes. Early examples are dictation systems and text-to-speech tools that convert between spoken and written language. These technologies are already successful in limited areas but within the next few years they will reach full maturity, opening up much larger markets. They will be complemented by reliable conversion from spoken or written language into sign language and vice versa. LT will also be utilised for improved methods of supported communication and for conversion of everyday language into greatly simplified language for special types of disabilities.

5.3 COMMUNICATION WITH TECHNOLOGY

Through language technology, human language will become the primary medium for communication between people and technology. Today's voice-control interfaces to smartphones and search engines are just the modest start of overcoming the communication barrier between humankind and the non-human part of the world.

This world consists of plants, animals, and other natural and man-made objects. The realm of man-made things ranges from small, simple objects to machines, appliances, and vehicles and more complex units such as robots, airplanes, buildings, traffic systems, and even entire cities. The artificially created world also consists of information and knowledge contained in books, films, recordings, and digital storage. Virtually all information and knowledge will soon be available in digital form and as a result the volumes of information about the world are growing exponentially. The result is a gigantic distributed digital model of our world that is continuously growing in complexity and fidelity. Through massive networking of this information and the linking of open data, this "second world" is getting more useful as a resource for information, planning, and knowledge creation.

We have a clear distinction between intelligent beings (humans, artificial agents with some autonomous behaviour) and all other kinds of objects. We can easily communicate with people and we would like to communicate with computers and robots, but we usually do not feel a pressing need to speak with a cup or with a power drill. However, as more and more products are equipped with sensors, processors, and information services such as

descriptions, specifications, or manuals, this expectation is changing rapidly: only a few years ago the idea of talking to a car to access key functions would have seemed absurd, yet it is now commonplace. Many everyday objects are already connected to the internet (Internet of Things) or at least represented on the web (Web of Things) – eventually we can and will communicate with such objects.

Depending on the function, complexity, relevance, and autonomy of man-made objects, the nature of desired communication can vary widely. Some objects will come with interesting information, often represented in the second world, that we would like to query and explore (such as manuals and consumer information). Other objects will provide information on their state and will have their own individual memory that can be queried. Objects than can perform actions, such as vehicles and appliances, will accept and carry out voice commands.

Recently the concept of a personal digital assistant has increased in popularity due to Siri on the iPhone and a similar product by Google. We will soon see much more sophisticated virtual personalities with expressive voices, faces, and gestures. They will become an interface to any information provided online. An assistant could speak about or even to machines, locations, the weather, the Empire State Building, or the London Stock Exchange. The metaphor of a personal assistant is powerful and extremely useful, since such an assistant can be made sensitive to the user's preferences, habits, moods, and goals. It can even be made aware of socio-emotional signals and learn appropriate reactions from experience.

Realising this ambitious vision will require a dedicated and thoughtfully planned massive effort in research and innovation. By the year 2020 we could have a highly personalised, socially aware and interactive virtual assistant. Having been trained on the user's behaviour, digital information, and communication space, it will proactively offer valuable unrequested advice. Voice, gender, language, and mentality of the virtual character could be adjusted to the user's preferences. The agent will be able to speak in the language and dialect of the user but also digest information in other natural and artificial languages and formats. The assistant will translate or interpret without the user even needing to request it. In the future, many providers of information about products, services, or touristic sites will try to present their information with a specific look and feel. The personality and functionality of the interface may also depend on the user type: there may be special interfaces for children, foreigners, and persons with disabilities.

By the year 2020 there will be a competitive landscape of intelligent interfaces to all kinds of objects and services employing human language and other modes, such as manual and facial gestures, for effective communication. Depending on the needed functions and available information, language coverage will range from simple commands to sophisticated dialogues. Many interface services will be offered as customisable cloud-based middleware, while others may be completely customised. The technologies needed for such interfaces to machines, objects, and locations are all part of the socially aware virtual assistant, so our priority theme also proposes creating enabling technologies for other interface products.

Two large application domains stand out in their demands and need for additional technologies: robotics and knowledge services.

Although robots have already taken over large parts of industrial production, the real era of robots is still ahead of us. Within this decade, specialised mobile robots will be deployed for personal services, rescue missions, household chores, and tasks of guarding and surveillance. Natural language is by far the best communication medium for natural human-robot interaction. By 2020 we will have robots around us that can communicate with us in human language, but their user friendliness and acceptance will largely depend on progress in LT research in the coming years. Since human language is very elaborate when speaking about perception, motion, and action in space and time, interaction with the physical world poses enormous challenges to LT. Some of these challenges can be addressed within the priority theme of the digital assistant, but without additional LT research in robotics, the communication skills of robots will lag behind their physical capabilities for a long time.

Communication with knowledge services raises a different set of problems: the inherent complexity of the represented knowledge requires considerable advances in technology. This complexity arises from the intricate structures of the subject domains and the richness of linguistic expressivity, in particular the great variety of options to implicitly or explicitly express the same fact or question. Moreover, much of the information that we can learn from a text stands between the lines. For us it follows from the text, but for language technology it needs to be derived by applying reasoning mechanisms and inference rules along with large amounts of explicitly encoded knowledge about the world.

From watching Star Trek, we have come to expect that one day we will be able to just say "Computer," followed by any question. As long as an answer can be found or derived from the accumulated knowledge of mankind, it will come back in a matter of milliseconds. In the Jeopardy game show, IBM's Watson was able to find correct answers that none of its human competitors could provide, which might lead one, erroneously, to think that the problem of automatic question answering is solved. Undoubtedly Watson is a great achievement that demonstrates the power of LT, but some of the questions that were too hard for the human quiz champions were actually rather easy for a machine that has ready access to handbooks, decades of news, lexicons, dictionaries, bibles, databases, and the entire Wikipedia. With clever lookup and selection mechanisms for the extraction of answers, Watson could actually find the right responses without a full analysis of the questions.

Outside the realm of quiz shows, however, most questions that people might ask cannot be answered by today's technology, even if it has access to the entire web, because they require a certain degree of understanding of both the question and the passages containing potential answers. Research on automatic question answering and textual inferencing progresses is progressing rapidly and by 2020 we will be able to use internet services that can answer huge numbers of non-trivial questions. One prerequisite for this envisaged knowledge access through natural communication are novel technologies for offline processing of large knowledge repositories and massive volumes of other meaningful data which will be discussed in the following subsection.

5.4 PROCESSING KNOWLEDGE AND INFORMATION

Most knowledge on the web, by far, is formulated in human language. However, machines cannot yet automatically interpret the texts containing this knowledge. Machines can interpret knowledge represented in databases but databases are too simple in structure to express complex concepts and their relations. The logical formalisms of semanticists that were designed to cope with the complexity of human thought, on the other hand, proved too unwieldy for practical computation. Therefore computational logicians developed simpler logic representation languages as a compromise between desired expressivity and required computability. In these languages, knowledge engineers can create formal models of knowledge domains and ontologies, describing the concepts of the domains by their properties and their relations to other concepts. Ontologies enable knowledge engineers to specify which things, people, and places in the world belong to which concepts. Such a domain model can be queried like a database. Its contents can be automatically analysed and modified.

The encoding of knowledge seemed to be a promising alternative to the current web, so that the vision of the Semantic Web was born. Its main bottleneck, however, remains the problem of knowledge acquisition. The intellectual creation of domain models turned out to be an extremely demanding and time-consuming task, requiring well-trained specialists that prepare new ontologies from scratch or base their work on existing taxonomies, ontologies, or categorisation systems. It is unrealistic to expect typical authors of web content to encode knowledge in Semantic Web languages based on description logics, nor will there be any affordable services for the manual conversion of large volumes of content.

Since LT did not have any means for automatically interpreting texts, language technologists had developed methods for extracting at least some relevant pieces of information. A rather simple task is the recognition of all person and company names, time and date expressions, locations and monetary expressions (named entity extraction). Much harder is the recognition of relations such as the one between company and customer, company and employee, or inventor and invention. Even more difficult are many-place relations such as the four-place relation of a wedding between groom and bride at a certain date and time. Events are typical cases of relations. However, events can have many more components, such as the causes, victims and circumstances of accidents. Although research in this area is advancing, a reliable recognition of relations is not yet possible. Information extraction can also be used for learning and populating ontologies. Texts and pieces of texts can be annotated with extracted data. These metadata can serve as a bridge between the semantic portions of the web and the traditional web of unstructured data. LT is indispensable for the realisation of a semantic web.

LT can perform many other tasks in the processing of knowledge and information. It can sort, categorise, catalogue, and filter content and it can deliver the data for data mining in texts. LT can automatically connect web documents with meaningful hyperlinks and it can produce summaries of larger collections of texts. Opinion mining and sentiment analysis can find out what people think about products, personalities, or problems and analyse their feelings about such topics.

Another class of techniques is needed for connecting between different media in the multimedia content of the web. Some of the needed tasks are annotating pictures, videos, and sound recordings with metadata, interlinking multimedia files with texts, semantic linking and searching in films and video content, and cross-media analytics, including cross-media summarisation.

In the next few years we will see considerable advances for all these techniques. For large parts of research and application development, language processing and knowledge processing will merge. The most dramatic innovations will draw from progress in multiple subfields. The predicted and planned use of language and knowledge technologies for social intelligence applications, one of our three priority areas, will involve text and speech analytics, translation, summarisation, opinion mining, sentiment analysis, and several other technologies. If the planned massive endeavour in this direction can be realised, it will not only result in a new quality of collective decision-making in business and politics. In 2020, LT will enable forms of knowledge evolution, knowledge transmission, and knowledge exploitation that speed up scientific, social, and cultural development. The effects for other knowledge-intensive application areas such as business intelligence, scientific knowledge discovery, and multimedia production will be immense.

5.5 LEARNING LANGUAGE

Soon almost every citizen on Earth will learn a second language, many will learn a third. A few will go beyond this by acquiring additional languages. Learning a language after the period of early childhood is hard. It is very different from acquiring scientific knowledge because it requires repetitious practicing by actual language use. The more natural the use, the more effective the practice is.

IT products that help to ease and speed up language learning have a huge market. Already today, the software market for computer-assisted language learning (CALL) is growing at a fast rate. While current products are helpful complements to traditional language instruction, they are still limited in functionality because the software cannot reliably analyse and critique the language produced by the learner. This is true for written language and even more so for spoken utterances. Software producers are trying to circumvent the problem by greatly restricting the expected responses of the user, something that helps for many exercises, but it still rules out the ideal interactive CALL application: an automatic dialogue partner ready around the clock for error-free conversation on many topics. Such software would analyse and critique the learner's errors and adapts its dialogue to the learner's problems and progress. LT cannot yet provide such functionality.

This lack of flexibility is the reason why research on CALL applications has not yet come into full bloom. As research on language analysis, understanding and dialogue systems progresses, we predict a boom in this promising and commercially attractive application area. Research toward the missing technologies is covered by our priority themes. We expect a strong increase in CALL research between 2015 and 2020.

5.6 LEARNING THROUGH LANGUAGE

Since most K-12, academic, and vocational instruction happens through language, spoken in classroom and read in textbooks, LT can and will play a central role in learning. Currently LT is already applied at a few places in the preparation of multiple-choice tests and in the assessment of learners' essays. As soon as dialogue systems can robustly conduct nearly error-free dialogues based on provided knowledge, research can design ideal tutoring systems. But long before LT research will reach this point, we will be able to create systems that test for knowledge by asking questions and that provide knowledge to the learner by answering questions. Thus even adaptive loops of analytic knowledge diagnosis and customised knowledge transmission as they form the core of an effective learning system will become possible through LT. Knowledge structuring and question answering is covered by our priority themes. The transfer to research and development toward educational applications should happen through close cooperation with the active research scene in e-learning. We predict that e-learning technology will have become much more effective and learner-friendly by that time through the integration of advanced LT.

5.7 CREATIVE CONTENTS AND CREATIVE WORK

A major cost issue for European tv and film production is subtitling and dubbing [47]. Whereas some countries with multiple official languages or with strict legislation mandating subtitling or sign-language display have a long tradition in providing these services, producers in many other countries still leave all subtitling and dubbing to importing distributors or media partners. With a single digital market, the increase in productions for multiple language communities, and with the strengthening of inclusion policies [48], the demand for fast and cost-effective subtitling and dubbing will grow significantly.

The automatic translation of subtitles is easier than the translation of newspaper articles because of shorter and simpler sentences in spoken language. Some commercial services have already started using machine translation for subtitles and audio description. If monolingual subtitling becomes the norm demanded by law, automated subtitle translation could be deployed at large scale.

Open challenges are the automatic production of sign-language translations and dubbing. Especially automatic dubbing will be a hard task since it requires the interpretation of the intonation in the source language, the generation of the adequate intonation in the target language, and finally lip synchronisation. An easier method would be automatic voice-over. In 2020 we will see wide use of automatic subtitling and first successful examples of automatic voice over for a few languages.

Language can also be a medium for creative work. In fine arts, creation mainly happens by a direct production of visual objects or images in two or three-dimensional space through drawing, constructing, painting, or photographing. In creative writing, the creation happens in language. In many other areas of creative work, the creation happens *through* languages, ranging from musical notation to programming languages. Here the created work is specified in some suitable notation. Often natural language is used, for instance in the formulation of scripts for movies or in the design of processes or services.

In computer science, the idea of writing programmes in natural language is as old as programming itself. This approach would require the translation of natural language into a programming language. However, the inherent ambiguity, vagueness and richness of natural language has remained a major problem. Computer scientists have created a number of easily learnable scripting languages, whose syntax resembles simple sentence structures of English. We expect that the concept of programming in natural language will bear fruit through progress in the semantic interpretation of natural language with respect to formal ontologies. The ontology-based interpretation of natural language statements will also permit the specification of processes, services, and objects which will then be translated into formal descriptions and finally into actions, models, workflows or physical objects. By 2020 we can expect examples of natural language scripting and specification in a few application areas.

5.8 DIAGNOSIS AND THERAPY

Psychological and medical conditions affecting language are among the most severe impairments from which people can suffer. Deficiencies in language can also be strong indicators for other conditions that are harder to detect directly, such as damage to the brain, nerves, or articulatory system. LT has been utilised for diagnosing the type and extent of brain damage after strokes. Since diagnosis and therapy are time critical for successful recovery of brain functions, software can support the immediate detection and treatment of stroke effects. Language technology can also be applied to the diagnosis and therapy of aphasia resulting from causes other than strokes, e. g., from infections or physical injuries.

Another application area is the diagnosis and therapy of innate or acquired speech impairments, especially in children. Dyslexia is a widespread condition affecting skills in reading and orthography. Some effects of dyslexia can be greatly reduced by appropriate training methods. Recent advances in the development of software for the therapy of dyslexia give rise to the hope that specialised CALL systems for different age groups and types of dyslexia will help to treat this condition early and effectively.

Technologies for augmentative alternative communication can perform an important function in therapy since any improvement of communication for language-impaired patients opens new ways for the treatment of causal or collateral conditions. Expected progress in LT, together with advances in miniaturisation and prosthetics, will open new ways for helping people who cannot naturally enjoy the benefits of communication.

5.9 LT AS A KEY-ENABLING TECHNOLOGY

The wide range of novel or improved applications in our shared vision represent only a fragment of the countless opportunities for LT to change our work and everyday life. Language-proficient technology will enable or enhance applications wherever language is present. It will change the production, management, and use of patents, legal contracts, medical reports, recipes, technical descriptions, and scientific texts, and it will permit many new voice applications such as automatic services for the submission of complaints and suggestions, for accepting orders, and for counselling in customer-care, e-government, education, community services, etc.

With so many applications and application areas, we may be tempted to doubt that there is a common technology core. And indeed there has been a trend of excessive diversification in LT software development and many tools can only be used for only one purpose. This limitation is different from the way humans learn their language: once we have learned our mother tongue we can easily obtain new skills, always employing the core knowledge acquired during childhood. We learn to read, write, skim texts, summarise, outline, proof-read, edit, and translate.

Currently we are witnessing a promising trend in LT giving rise to hope for faster progress. Instead of relying on highly specialised components, powerful core technologies are reused for many applications. We can now compose lists of components and tools that we need for every language since these will be adapted for and integrated into many applications. In addition, we have also identified lists of core data (such as text and speech corpora) and language descriptions (such as lexicons, thesauri and grammars) needed for a wide spectrum of purposes.

In IT we can differentiate between application technologies, such as credit-card readers, and enabling technologies, such as microprocessors, that are needed for multiple types of applications. In hardware technology, certain key-enabling technologies have been identified. These are indispensable for projected essential progress (e. g., nanotechnology, microelectronics and semiconductors, biotechnology). Similar key-enabling technologies exist on the software side, such as database technology or net-

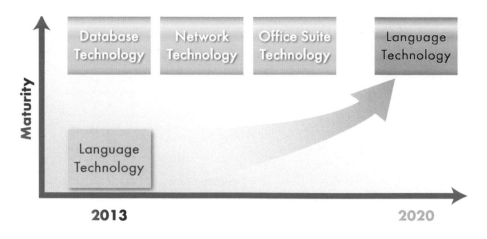

8: By the year 2020, Language Technology will have become a key enabling technology

work technology. Considering the broad range of LT-enabled applications and their potential impact on business and society, LT is certainly becoming a key enabling technology for future generations of IT (see Figure 8). In contrast to some of the other key enabling technologies listed above, Europe has not yet lost a leadership role in the field. There is no reason to be discouraged or even paralysed by the strong evidence of interest and expertise on the side of major commercial players in the US. In software markets the situation can change fast.

If Europe does not take a decisive stand for a substantial commitment to LT research and innovation in the years to come, we may as well give up any ambition in the future of IT altogether because there is no other software sector in which European research can benefit from a similar combination of existing competitive competence, recognised economic potential, acknowledged societal needs, and determined political obligation toward our unique wealth of languages.

LANGUAGE TECHNOLOGY 2020: THE META-NET PRIORITY RESEARCH THEMES

6.1 INTRODUCTION

For decades it has been obvious that one of the last remaining frontiers of IT is still separating our rapidly evolving technological world of mobile devices, computers and the internet from the most precious and powerful asset of mankind, the human mind, the only system capable of thought, knowledge and emotion. Although we use computers to write, telephones to chat and the web to search for knowledge, IT has no direct access to the meaning, purpose and sentiment behind our trillions of written and spoken words. This is why technology is unable to summarise a text, answer a question, respond to a letter and to translate reliably. In many cases it cannot even correctly pronounce a simple English sentence.

Visionaries such as Ray Kurzweil, Marvin Minsky and Bill Gates have long predicted that this border would eventually be overcome by artificial intelligence including language understanding whereas science fiction such as the Star Trek TV series suggested attractive ways in which technology would change our lives, by establishing the fantastic concept of an invisible computer that you have a conversation with and that is able to react to the most difficult commands and also of technology that can reliably translate any human and non-human language.

Many companies had started much too early to invest in language technology research and development and then lost faith after a long period without any tangible progress. During the years of apparent technological standstill, however, research continued to conquer new ground. The results were a deeper theoretical understanding of language, better machine-readable dictionaries, thesauri and grammars, specialised efficient language processing algorithms, hardware with increased computing power and storage capacities, large volumes of digitised text and speech data and new methods of statistical language processing that could exploit language data for learning hidden regularities governing our language use.

We do not yet possess the complete know-how for unleashing the full potential of language technology as essential research results are still missing. Nevertheless, the speed of research keeps increasing and even small improvements can already be exploited for innovative products and services that are commercially viable. We are witnessing a chain of new products for a variety of applications entering the market in rapid succession.

These applications tend to be built on dedicated computational models of language processing that are specialised for a certain task. People, on the other hand, apply the basic knowledge of the language they have acquired during the first few years of their socialisation, throughout their lives to many different tasks of varying complexity such as reading, writing, skimming, summarising, studying, editing, arguing, teaching. They even use this knowledge for the learning of additional languages. After people have obtained proficiency in a second language, they can already translate simple sentences more fluently than many machine translation systems, whereas truly adequate and stylistically acceptable translation is a highly skillful art gained by special training.

G. Rehm and H. Uszkoreit (eds.), *META-NET Strategic Research Agenda for Multilingual Europe 2020*, White Paper Series, DOI: 10.1007/978-3-642-36349-8_6, © The Author(s) 2013

Today, no text technology software can translate and check for grammatical correctness and no speech technology software could recognise all the sentences it can read aloud if they were spoken by people in their normal voices. But increasingly we observe a reuse of core components and language models for a wide variety of purposes. It started with dictionaries, spell checkers and text-to-speech tools. Google Translate, Apple's Siri and IBM Watson still do not use the same technologies for analysing and producing language, because the generic processing components are simply not powerful enough to meet their respective needs. But many advanced research systems already utilise the same tools for syntactic analysis. This process is going to continue.

In ten years or less, basic language proficiency is going to be an integral component of any advanced IT. It will be available to any user interface, service and application development. Additional language skills for semantic search, knowledge discovery, human-technology communication, text analytics, language checking, e-learning, translation and other applications will employ and extend the basic proficiency. The shared basic language competence will ensure consistency and interoperability among services. Many adaptations and extensions will be derived and improved through sample data and interaction with people by powerful machine learning techniques.

In the envisaged big push toward realising this vision by massive research and innovation, the technology community is faced with three enormous challenges:

1. *Richness and diversity.* A serious challenge is the sheer number of languages, some closely related, others distantly apart. Within a language, technology has to deal with numerous dialects, sociolects, registers, professional jargons, genres and slangs.

2. *Depth and meaning.* Understanding language is a complex process. Human language is not only the key to knowledge and thought, it also cannot be interpreted without certain shared knowledge and active inference. Computational language proficiency needs semantic technologies.

3. *Multimodality and grounding.* Human language is embedded in our daily activities. It is combined with other modes and media of communication. It is affected by beliefs, desires, intentions and emotions and it affects all of these. Successful interactive language technology requires models of embodied and adaptive human interaction with people, technology and other parts of the world.

It is fortunate for research and economy that the only way to effectively tackle the three challenges involves submitting the evolving technology continuously to the growing demands and practical stress tests of real world applications. Google's Translate, Apple's Siri, Autonomy's text analytics and scores of other products demonstrate that there are plenty of commercially viable applications for imperfect technologies. Only a continuous stream of technological innovation can provide the economic pull forces and the evolutionary environments for the realisation of the grand vision.

In the remainder of the Chapter, we propose five major action lines of research and innovation:

- Three priority themes connected with powerful application scenarios that can drive research and innovation. These will demonstrate novel technologies in attractive show-case solutions of high economic and societal impact. They will open up numerous new business opportunities for European language-technology and -service providers.

- A steadily evolving system of shared, collectively maintained interoperable core technologies and resources for the languages of Europe and selected economically relevant languages of its partners. These will ensure that our languages will be sufficiently supported and represented in the next generations of IT.

- A pan-European language technology service platform for supporting research and innovation by testing and showcasing research results, integrating various services even including professional human services will allow SME providers to offer component and end-user services, and share and utilise tools, components and data resources.

The three priority research themes are:

- **Translingual Cloud** – generic and specialised federated cloud services for instantaneous reliable spoken and written translation among all European and major non-European languages.
- **Social Intelligence** – understanding and dialogue within and across communities of citizens, customers, clients and consumers to enable e-participation and more effective processes for preparing, selecting and evaluating collective decisions.
- **Socially Aware Interactive Assistants** – socially aware assistants that learn and adapt and that provide proactive and interactive support tailored to specific situations, locations and goals of the user through verbal and non-verbal multimodal communication.

These priority themes have been designed with the aim of turning our vision into reality and to letting Europe benefit from a technological revolution that will overcome barriers of understanding between people of different languages, between people and technology and between people and the knowledge of mankind. The themes connect societal needs with LT applications and roadmaps for the organisation of research, development and innovation. The priority themes cover the main functions of language: storing, sharing and using of information and knowledge, as well as improving social interaction among humans and enabling social interaction between humans and technology. As multilingualism is at the core of European culture and becoming a global norm, one theme is devoted to overcoming language barriers.

The three themes have been selected in a complex process (see Appendix C, p. 80 ff.) to ensure the needed market pull, the appropriate performance demands, the realistic testing environments and public interest. The themes represent a mix of applications with respect to the various user communities such as small businesses, large enterprises, public administration and the public at large.

6.2 PRIORITY THEME 1: TRANSLINGUAL CLOUD

6.2.1 Solutions for the EU Society

The goal is a multilingual European society, in which all citizens can use any service, access all knowledge, enjoy all media and control any technology *in their mother tongues*. This will be a world in which written and spoken communication is not hindered anymore by language barriers and in which even specialised high-quality translation will be affordable.

The citizen, the professional, the organisation, or the software application in need of cross-lingual communication will use a single, simple access point for channelling text or speech through a gateway that will instantly return the translations into the requested languages in the required quality and desired format.

Behind this access point will be a network of generic and special-purpose services combining automatic translation or interpretation, language checking, post-editing, as well as human creativity and quality assurance, where needed, for achieving the demanded quality. For high-volume base-line quality the service will be free for use but it will offer extensive business opportunities for a wide range of service and technology providers.

Selected components of this ubiquitous service are:

- use and provision platform for providers of computer-supported top-quality human translation, multilingual text authoring and quality assurance by experts

- trusted service centres: certified service providers fulfilling highest standards for privacy, confidentiality and security of source data and translations

- quality upscale models: services permitting instant quality upgrades if the results of the requested service levels do not yet fulfil the quality requirements

- domain, task and genre specialisation models

- translingual spaces: dedicated locations for ambient interpretation. Meeting rooms equipped with acoustic technology for accurate directed sound sensing and emission

6.2.2 Novel Research Approaches and Targeted Breakthroughs

The main reason why high-quality machine translation (HQMT) has not been systematically addressed yet seems to be the Zipfian distribution of issues in MT: some improvements, the "low-hanging fruit", can be harvested with moderate effort in a limited amount of time. Yet, many more resources and a more fundamental, novel scientific approach – that eventually runs across several projects and also calls – are needed for significant and substantial improvements that cover the phenomena and problems that make up the Zipfian long tail. This is an obstacle in particular for individual research centres and SMEs given their limited resources and planning horizon. Although recent progress in MT has already led to many new applications of this technology, radically different approaches are needed to accomplish the ambitious goal of this research including a true quality breakthrough. Among these new research approaches are:

- Systematic concentration on quality barriers, i. e., on obstacles for high quality

- A unified dynamic-depth weighted-multidimensional quality assessment model with task profiling

- Strongly improved automatic quality estimation

- Inclusion of translation professionals and enterprises in the entire research and innovation process

- Improved statistical models that extract more dependencies from the data

- Ergonomic work environments for computer-supported creative top-quality human translation and multilingual text authoring

- Semantic translation paradigm by extending statistical translation with semantic data such as linked open data, ontologies including semantic models of processes and textual inference models

- Exploitation of strong monolingual analysis and generation methods and resources

- Modular combinations of specialised analysis, generation and transfer models, permitting accommodation of registers and styles (including user-generated content) and also enabling translation within a language (e. g., between specialists and laypersons).

The expected breakthroughs will include:

- High-quality text translation and reliable speech translation (including a modular analysis-transfer-generation translation technology that facilitates reuse and constant improvement of modules)

- Seemingly creative translation skills by analogy-driven transfer models

- Automatic subtitling and voice over of films

- Ambient translation

6.2.3 Solution and Realisation

The technical solutions will benefit from new trends in IT such as software as a service, cloud computing, linked open data and semantic web, social networks, crowdsourcing etc. For MT, a combination of translation brokering on a large scale and translation on demand is promising. The idea is to streamline the translation process so that it becomes simpler to use and more transpar-

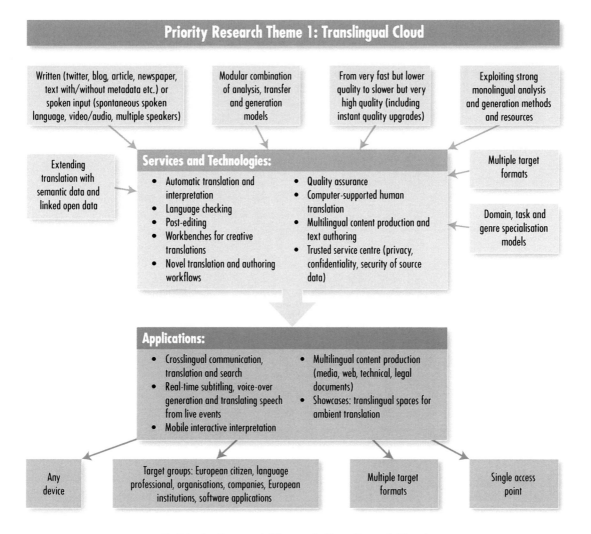

Priority Research Theme 1: Translingual Cloud

Written (twitter, blog, article, newspaper, text with/without metadata etc.) or spoken input (spontaneous spoken language, video/audio, multiple speakers)

Modular combination of analysis, transfer and generation models

From very fast but lower quality to slower but very high quality (including instant quality upgrades)

Exploiting strong monolingual analysis and generation methods and resources

Extending translation with semantic data and linked open data

Services and Technologies:
- Automatic translation and interpretation
- Language checking
- Post-editing
- Workbenches for creative translations
- Novel translation and authoring workflows

- Quality assurance
- Computer-supported human translation
- Multilingual content production and text authoring
- Trusted service centre (privacy, confidentiality, security of source data)

Multiple target formats

Domain, task and genre specialisation models

Applications:
- Crosslingual communication, translation and search
- Real-time subtitling, voice-over generation and translating speech from live events
- Mobile interactive interpretation

- Multilingual content production (media, web, technical, legal documents)
- Showcases: translingual spaces for ambient translation

Any device

Target groups: European citizen, language professional, organisations, companies, European institutions, software applications

Multiple target formats

Single access point

9: Priority Research Theme 1: Translingual Cloud

ent for the end user, and at the same time respects important factors such as subject domain, language, style, genre, corporate requirements and user preferences. Technically, what is required is maximum interoperability of all components (corpora, processing tools, terminology, knowledge, maybe even translation models) and a cloud or server/service farm of specialised language technology services for different needs (text and media types, domains, etc.) offered by SMEs, large companies or research centres.

A platform has to be designed and implemented for the resource and evaluation demands of large-scale collaborative MT research. An initial inventory of language tools and resources as well as extensive experience in shared tasks and evaluation has been obtained in several EU-funded projects. Together with LSPs, a common service layer supporting research workflows on HQMT must be established. As third-party (customer) data is needed for realistic development and evaluation, intellectual property rights and legal issues must be taken into account from the onset. The infrastructures to be built include service clouds with trusted service centres, interfaces for services (APIs), workbenches for creative translations, novel translation workflows (and improved links to content production and authoring) and showcases such as ambient and embedded translation.

Research Priority	Phase 1: 2013-2014	Phase 2: 2015-2017	Phase 3: 2018-2020
Immediate affordable translation in any needed quality level (from sufficient to high)	Development of necessary monolingual language tools (analysis, generation) driven by MT needs; exploitation of novel ML techniques for MT purposes, using large LR and semantic resources, including Linked Open Data and other naturally occuring semantic and knowledge resources (re-purposing for MT and NLP use); experiment with novel metrics, automated, human-centered, or hybrid; use EU languages, identify remaining gaps (LR resources, tools)	Concentrate on HQMT systems using results of Phase 1; deepen development of MT-related monolingual tools; employ novel techniques aimed at HQMT, combination of systems, domain adaptation, cross-language adaptation; develop showcases for novel translation workflow; use novel metrics identified as correlated with the aims of HQMT; continue development on EU languages, identify needs for non-EU languages (MT-related) and their gaps	Deployment of MT systems in particular applications requiring HQMT, such as technology export, government and public information systems, private services, medical applications etc., using novel translation workflows where appropriate; application- and user-based evaluation driven engagement of core and supplemental technologies; coverage of EU languages and other languages important for EU business and policy
Delivering multimedia content in any language (captioning, subtitling, dubbing)	Multi-media system prototypes, combining language, speech, image and video analysis; employing novel techniques (machine learning, cross-fertilisation of features across media types); targeted evaluation metrics for system quality assessment related to MT; aimed at EU languages with sufficient resources; data collection effort to support multi-media analysis	Prototype applications in selected domains, such as public service (parliament recordings, sports events, legal proceedings) and other applications (tv archives or movie delivery, online services at content providers); continued effort at multimedia analysis, adding languages as resources become available	Deployment of large-scale applications for multi-media content delivery, public and/or private, in selected domains; development of online services for captioning, subtitling, dubbing, including on-demand translation); new languages for outside-of-the-EU delivery, continued improvement of EU languages
Cross-lingual knowledge management and linked open data	Publication of multilingual language resources as linked open data as well as linking of resources across languages; develop ontology translation components that can localise ontologies and linked datasets to different languages	Develop an ecosystem of NLP tools and services that leverage the existing multilingual resources on linked open data; develop new generation of MT technology that can profit from semantic data and linked open data	Develop methods that allow querying linked open data in different languages
Avantgarde functionalities	Consecutive interpretation and translation	Synchronous interpretation and translation	Translingual collaborative spaces

10: Priority Theme 1 – Translingual Cloud: Preliminary Roadmap

6.2.4 Impact

HQMT in the cloud will ensure and extend the value of the digital information space in which everyone can contribute in her own language and be understood by members of other language communities. It will assure that diversity will no longer be a challenge, but a welcome enrichment for Europe both socially and economically. Based on the new technology, language-transparent web and language-transparent media will help realise a truly multilingual mode of online and media interaction for every citizen regardless of age, education, profession, cultural background, language proficiency or technical skills. Showcase applications areas are:

- Multilingual content production (media, web, technical, legal documents)
- Cross-lingual communication, document translation and search
- Real-time subtitling and translating speech from live events
- Mobile interactive interpretation for business, social services, and security
- Translation workspaces for online services

6.2.5 Organisation of Research

Several very large cooperating and competing lead projects will share an infrastructure for evaluation, resources (data and base technologies), and communication. Mechanisms for reducing or terminating partner involvements and for adding new partners or subcontracted contributors should provide the needed flexibility. A number of smaller projects, including national and regional projects, will provide building blocks for particular languages, tasks, component technologies or resources. A special scheme will be designed for involving EC-funding, member states, industrial associations, and language communities.

Two major phases from 2015 to mid 2017 and from mid 2017 to 2020 are foreseen. Certain services such as multilingual access to web-information across European languages should be transferred to implementation and testing at end of phase 2017. Internet-based real-time speech translation for a smaller set of languages will also get into service at this time as well as HQMT for selected domains and tasks. A major mid-term revision with a thorough analytical evaluation will provide a possible breakpoint for replanning or termination.

A close cooperation of language technology and professional language services is planned. In order to overcome the quality boundaries we need to identify and understand the quality barriers. Professional translators and post-editors are required whose judgements and corrections will provide insights for the analytical approach and data for the bootstrapping methodology. The cooperation scheme of research, commercial services and commercial translation technology is planned as a symbiosis since language service professionals or advanced students in translation studies or related programmes working with and for the developing technology will at the same time be the first test users analytically monitored by the evaluation schemes. This symbiosis will lead to a better interplay of research and innovation.

Although the research strand will focus on advances in translation technology for innovation in the language and translation service sector, a number of other science, technology and service areas need to be integrated into the research from day one. Some technology areas such as speech technologies, language checking, authoring systems, analytics, generation and content management systems need to be represented by providers of state-of-the-art commercial products.

Supporting research and innovation in LT should be accompanied by policy making in the area of multilingualism, but also in digital accessibility. Overcoming language barriers can greatly influence the future of the EU.

Solutions for better communication and for access to content in the users' native languages would reaffirm the role of the EC to serve the needs of the EU citizens. A connection to the infrastructure programme CEF could help to speed up the transfer of research results to badly needed services for the European economy and public.

At the same time, use cases should cover areas in which the European social and societal needs massively overlap with business opportunities to achieve funding investment that pays back, ideally public-private partnerships. Concerted activities sharing resources such as error corpora or test suites and challenges or shared tasks in carefully selected areas should be offered to accelerate innovation breakthrough and market-readiness for urgently needed technologies.

6.3 PRIORITY THEME 2: SOCIAL INTELLIGENCE AND E-PARTICIPATION

6.3.1 Solutions for the EU Society

The central goal behind this theme is to use information technology and the digital content of the web for improving effectiveness and efficiency of decision-making in business and society.

The quality, speed and acceptance of individual and collective decisions is the single main factor for the success of social systems such as enterprises, public services, communities, states and supranational organisations. The growing quantity and complexity of accessible relevant information poses a serious challenge to the efficiency and quality of decision processes. IT provides a wide range of instruments for intelligence applications. Business intelligence, military intelligence or security intelligence applications collect and pre-process decision-relevant information. Analytics programmes search the data for such information and decision support systems evaluate and sort the information and apply problem-specific decision rules. Although much of the most relevant information is contained in texts, text analytics programmes today only account for less than 1% of the more than 10 billion US$ business intelligence and analytics market. Because of their limited capabilities in interpreting texts, mainly business news, reports and press releases, their findings are still neither comprehensive nor reliable enough.

Social intelligence builds on improved text analytics methodologies but goes far beyond the analysis. One central goal is the analysis of large volumes of social media, comments, communications, blogs, forum postings etc. of citizens, customers, patients, employees, consumers and other stakeholder communities. Part of the analysis is directed to the status, opinions and acceptance associated with the individual information units. As the formation of collective opinions and attitudes is highly dynamic, new developments need to be detected and trends analysed. Emotions play an important part in individual actions such as voting, buying, supporting, donating and in collective opinion formation, the analysis of sentiment is a crucial component of social intelligence.

Social intelligence can also support collective deliberation processes. Today any collective discussion processes involving large numbers of participants are bound to become intransparent and incomprehensible rather fast. By recording, grouping, aggregating and counting opinion statements, pros and cons, supporting evidence, sentiments and new questions and issues, the discussion can be summarised and focussed. Decision processes can be structured, monitored, documented and visualised, so that joining, following and benefitting from them becomes much easier. The efficiency and impact of such processes can thus be greatly enhanced.

Since many collective discussions will involve participants in several countries, e. g., EU member states or enterprise locations, cross-lingual participation needs to be supported [32]. Special support will also be provided for

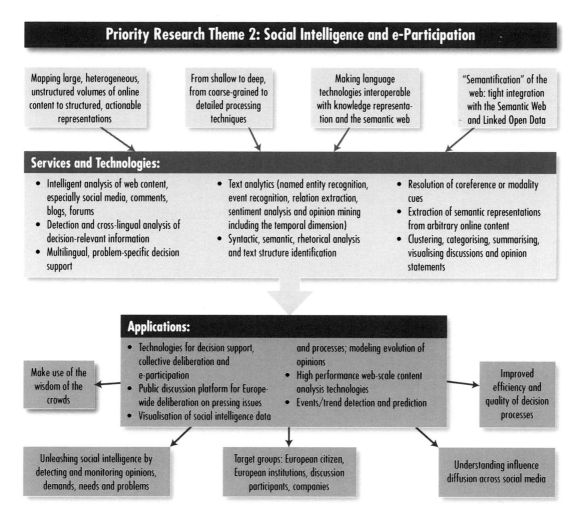

Priority Research Theme 2: Social Intelligence and e-Participation

Mapping large, heterogeneous, unstructured volumes of online content to structured, actionable representations

From shallow to deep, from coarse-grained to detailed processing techniques

Making language technologies interoperable with knowledge representation and the semantic web

"Semantification" of the web: tight integration with the Semantic Web and Linked Open Data

Services and Technologies:
- Intelligent analysis of web content, especially social media, comments, blogs, forums
- Detection and cross-lingual analysis of decision-relevant information
- Multilingual, problem-specific decision support

- Text analytics (named entity recognition, event recognition, relation extraction, sentiment analysis and opinion mining including the temporal dimension)
- Syntactic, semantic, rhetorical analysis and text structure identification

- Resolution of coreference or modality cues
- Extraction of semantic representations from arbitrary online content
- Clustering, categorising, summarising, visualising discussions and opinion statements

Applications:
- Technologies for decision support, collective deliberation and e-participation
- Public discussion platform for Europe-wide deliberation on pressing issues
- Visualisation of social intelligence data

and processes; modeling evolution of opinions
- High performance web-scale content analysis technologies
- Events/trend detection and prediction

Make use of the wisdom of the crowds

Improved efficiency and quality of decision processes

Unleashing social intelligence by detecting and monitoring opinions, demands, needs and problems

Target groups: European citizen, European institutions, discussion participants, companies

Understanding influence diffusion across social media

11: Priority Research Theme 2: Social Intelligence and e-Participation

participants not mastering certain group-specific or expert jargons and for participants with disabilities affecting their comprehension.

6.3.2 Novel Research Approaches and Targeted Breakthroughs

A key enabler will be language technologies that can map large, heterogeneous, and, to a large extent, unstructured volumes of online content to actionable representations that support decision making and analytics tasks. Such mappings can range from the relatively shallow to the relatively deep, encompassing for example coarse-grained topic classification at the document or paragraph level or

the identification of named entities, as well as in-depth syntactic, semantic and rhetorical analysis at the level of individual sentences and beyond (paragraph, chapter, text, discourse) or the resolution of co-reference or modality cues within and across sentences.

Technologies such as, e. g., information extraction, data mining, automatic linking and summarisation have to be made interoperable with knowledge representation and semantic web methods such as ontological engineering. Drawing expertise from related areas such as knowledge management, information sciences, or social sciences is a prerequisite to meet the challenge of modelling social intelligence [49]. The new research approach should target the bottleneck of knowledge engineering by:

- Semantification of the web: bridging between the semantic parts and islands of the web and the traditional web containing unstructured data;

- Merging and integrating textual data with social network and social media data, especially along the dimension of time;

- Aligning and making comparable different genres of content like mainstream-news, social media (blogs, twitter, facebook etc.), academic texts, archives etc.;

- Extracting semantic representations from social media content, i. e., creating representations for reasoning and inferencing;

- Taking metadata and multimedia data into account.

The following list contains specific targeted breakthroughs to be sought in this scenario:

- Social intelligence by detecting and monitoring opinions, demands, needs and problems;

- Detecting diversity of views, biases along different dimensions (e. g., demographic) etc. including temporal dimension (i. e., modelling evolution of opinions);

- Support for both decision makers and participants;

- Problem mining and problem solving;

- Support of collective deliberation and collective knowledge accumulation;

- Vastly improved approaches to sentiment detection and sentiment scoring (going beyond the approach that relies on a list of positive and negative keywords);

- Introducing genre-driven text and language-processing (different genres need to be processed differently);

- Personalised recommendations of e-participation topics to citizens;

- Proactive involvement in e-participation activities;

- Understanding influence diffusion across social media (identifying drivers of opinion spreading);

- More sophisticated methods for topic and event detection that are tightly integrated with the Semantic Web and Linked Open Data.

- Modelling content and opinion flows across social networks;

- Evaluation of methods by analytic/quantitative and sociological/qualitative means.

6.3.3 Solution and Realisation

Individual solutions should be assembled from a repository of generic monolingual and cross-lingual language technologies, packaging state-of-the-art techniques in robust, scalable, interoperable, and adaptable components that are deployed across sub-tasks and sub-projects, as well as across languages where applicable (e. g., when the implementation of a standard data-driven technique can be trained for individual languages). These methods need to be combined with powerful analytical approaches that can aggregate all relevant data to support analytic decision making and develop new access metaphors and task-specific visualisations.

By robust we mean technologically mature, engineered and scalable solutions that can perform high-throughput analysis of web data at different levels of depth and granularity in line with the requirements of their applications. Technology should be able to work with heterogeneous sources, ranging from unstructured (arbitrary text documents of any genre) to structured (ontologies, linked open data, databases).

To accomplish interoperability we suggest a strong semantic bias in the choice and design of interface representations: to the highest degree possible, the output (and at deeper levels of analysis also input) specifications of component technologies should be interpretable semantically, both in relation to natural language semantics (be it lexical, propositional, or referential) and extra-linguistic semantics (e. g., taxonomic world or domain knowledge). For example, grammatical analysis (which one may or may not decompose further into tagging, syntactic parsing, and semantic role labelling) should make available a sufficiently abstract, normalised, and detailed output, so that downstream processing can be accomplished without further recourse to knowledge about syntax. Likewise, event extraction or fine-grained, utterance-level opinion mining should operate in terms of formally interpretable representations that support notions of entailment and, ultimately, inference.

Finally, our adaptability requirement on component technologies addresses the inherent heterogeneity of information sources and communication channels to be processed. Even in terms of monolingual analysis only, linguistic variation across genres (ranging from carefully edited, formal publications to spontaneous and informal social media channels) and domains (as in subject matters) often calls for technology adaptation, where even relatively mature basic technologies (e. g., part-of-speech taggers) may need to be customised or re-trained to deliver satisfactory performance. Further taking into account variation across downstream tasks, web-scale language processing typically calls for different parameterisations and trade-offs (e. g., in terms of computational cost vs. breadth and depth of analysis) than an interactive self-help dialogue scenario. For these reasons, relevant trade-offs need to be documented empirically, and component technologies accompanied with methods and tools for adaptation and cost-efficient re-training, preferably in semi- and un-supervised settings.

The technical solutions needed include:

- Technologies for decision support, collective deliberation and e-participation.
- A large public discussion platform for Europe-wide deliberation on pressing issues such as energy policies, financial system, migration, natural disasters, etc.
- Visualisation of social intelligence-related data and processes for decision support (for politicians, health providers, manufacturers, or citizens).

- High-throughput, web-scale content analysis techniques that can process multiple different sources, ranging from unstructured to completely structured, at different levels of granularity and depth by allowing to trade-off depth for efficiency as required.
- Mining e-participation content for recommendations, summarisation and proactive engagement of less active parts of population.
- Detection and prediction of events and trends from content and social media networks.
- Extraction of knowledge and semantic integration of social content with sensory data and mobile devices (in near-real-time).
- Cross-lingual technology to increase the social reach and approach cross-culture understanding.

We suggest to structure the research along at least the six lines shown in Figure 12.

6.3.4 Impact

The 21st century presents us with multiple challenges including efficient energy consumption, global warming and financial crises. It is obvious that no single individual can provide answers to challenging problems such as these, nor will top-down imposed measures find social acceptance as solutions. Language technology will enable a paradigm shift in transnational public deliberation. The European Ombudsman recently realised [32] that there are problems and gaps in the way public debates and consultation are usually held in Europe – language technology can improve the situation altogether and bring about a paradigm shift in that regard.

The applications and technologies discussed in this section will change how business adapts and communicates with their customers. It will increase transparency in decision-making processes, e. g., in politics and at the same time give more power to the citizen. As a by-product, the citizens are encouraged to become better in-

Research Priority	Phase 1: 2013-2014	Phase 2: 2015-2017	Phase 3: 2018-2020
Social influence and incentives	Modelling social diversity of views across languages and cultures	Modelling social influence and incentives through game theoretic approaches using data from texts and social networks	Holistic modelling of society (or its segments) through observing a variety of data sources
Information tracking	Tracking dynamics of information diffusion across languages, cultures and media	Transforming textual and social network streams into actionable deep knowledge representations	Prediction of future events and identification of causal relationships from textual and social streams
Multimodal data processing	Joining textual data and social networks, including spatial and temporal dimensions	Joining textual and social data with unstructured sources like sensor data (smart cities), video, images, audio	Detecting inconsistencies, gaps and completeness of collected knowledge from textual and social sources
Visualisation and user interaction	Visualisation of textual and social dynamics	Adaptive human-computer interfaces boosting specific aims in interaction	Adaptive interaction systems for communication with the whole or parts of society
High-throughput analysis	Scalable processing of multimodal data (Big Data)	Real-time modelling and reasoning on massive textual and social streams	Algorithms and toolkits being able to deal with global scale analytics and reasoning with multimodal data
Knowledge-driven text analysis	Develop named-entity taggers that scale to entities described in linked open data resources; develop methods that exploit linked open data for improved disambiguation.	Develop a new generation of information extraction tools that are able to reliably extract from texts all semantic relations defined in, e. g., DBPedia	NLP systems are able to deal with linked open data and Semantic Web ontologies to analyse text at the meaning level and draw appropriate inferences

12: Priority Theme 2 – Social Intelligence and e-Participation: Preliminary Roadmap

formed in order to make use of their right to participate in a reasonable way. Powerful analytical methods will help European companies to optimise marketing strategies or foresee certain developments by extrapolating on the basis of current trends. Leveraging social intelligence for informed decision making is recognised as crucial in a wide range of contexts and scenarios:

- Organisations will better understand the needs, opinions, experiences, communication patterns, etc. of their actual and potential customers so that they can react quickly to new trends and optimise their marketing and customer communication strategies.

- Companies will get the desparately needed instruments to exploit the knowledge and expertise of their huge and diverse workforces, the wisdom of their own crowds, which are the most highly motivated and most closely affected crowds.

- Political decision makers will be able to analyse public deliberation and opinion formation processes in order to react swiftly to ongoing debates or important, sometimes unforeseen events.

- Citizens and customers get the opportunity (and necessary information) to participate and influence political, economic and strategic decisions of governments and companies, ultimately leading to more transparency of decision processes.

Thus, leveraging collective and social intelligence in developing new solutions to these 21st century challenges seems a promising approach in such domains where the complexity of the issues under discussion is beyond the purview of single individuals or groups.

The research and innovation will provide technological support for emerging new forms of issue-based, knowledge-enhanced and solution-centred participatory democracy involving large numbers of expert- and non-expert stakeholders distributed over large areas, using multiple languages. At the same time the resulting technologies will be applicable to smaller groups and also interpersonal communication as well, even though different dynamics of information exchange can be foreseen.

The research to be carried out and technologies to be developed in this priority theme will also have a big influence on the Big Data challenge and how we will make sense of huge amounts of data in the years to come. What we learn from processing language is the prime tool for processing the huge and intractable data streams that we will be confronted with in the near future.

6.3.5 Organisation of Research

Research in this area touches upon political as well as business interests and at the same time is scalable in reach from the regional to the European scale. Therefore, it is necessary to identify business opportunities and potential impact for society at different levels and to align EU level research with efforts on the national level. Furthermore, this priority theme calls for large-scale, incremental, and sustained development and innovation across multiple disciplines (especially language technology and semantic technologies) and, within each community, a certain degree of stacking and fusion of approaches. Therefore, research organisation needs to create strong incentives for early and frequent exchange of technologies among all players involved. A marketplace for generic component technologies and a service-

oriented infrastructure for adaptation and composition must be created, to balance performance-based steering and self-organisation among clusters of contributing players. In this ecosystem of technology providers and integrators, component uptake and measurable contributions against the targeted breakthrough of the priority theme at large should serve as central measures of success.

6.4 PRIORITY THEME 3: SOCIALLY AWARE INTERACTIVE ASSISTANTS

6.4.1 Solutions for the EU Society

Socially aware interactive assistants are conversational agents. Their socially-aware behaviour is a result of combining analysis methods for speech, non-verbal and semantic signals.

Now is the time to develop and make operational socially aware, multilingual assistants that support people interacting with their environment, including human-computer, human-artificial agent (or robot), and computer-mediated human-human interaction. The assistants must be able to act in various environments, both indoor (such as meeting rooms, offices, appartments), outdoor (streets, cities, transportation, roads) and virtual environments (such as the web, virtual worlds, games), and also be able to communicate, exchange information and understand other agents' intentions. They must be able to adapt to the user's needs and environment and have the capacity to learn incrementally from all interactions and other sources of information.

The ideal socially aware multilingual assistant can interact naturally with humans, in any language and modality. It can adapt and be personalised to individual communication abilities, including special needs (for the visual, hearing, or motor impaired), affections, or language proficiencies. It can recognise and generate speech incrementally and fluently. It is able to assess its performance and recover from errors. It can learn, personalise itself and forget. It can assist in language training and education, and provide synthetic multimedia information analytics. It recognises people's identity, and their gender, language or accent. If the agent is embodied in a robot, it can move, manipulate objects, and interact with people.

This priority theme includes several core components:

- Interacting naturally with humans (in communication, education, games, etc.) in an implicit (proactive) or explicit (spoken dialogue and/or gesticulation) manner based on robust analysis of human user identity, age, gender, verbal and nonverbal behaviour, and social context;

- Using language in connection with other communication modalities (visual, tactile, haptic);

- Conscious of its capabilities and self-learning;

- Exhibiting robust performance everywhere (indoor/outdoor, augmented reality);

- Overcoming handicap obstacles by means of suitable technologies (sign language understanding, assistive applications, etc.);

- Interacting naturally with and in groups (in social networks, with humans or artificial agents/robots);

- Exhibiting multilingual proficiency (speech-to-speech translation, interpretation in meetings and videoconferencing, cross-lingual information access);

- Referring to written support (transcription, close-captioning, reading machines, ebooks);

- Providing access to knowledge (answers to questions, shared knowledge in discussion);

- Providing personalised training (computer-assisted language learning, e-learning).

Initial steps in the right direction have already been taken – again, by US companies. Apple's intelligent assistant Siri is available on the iPhone, Google's interactive speech technologies can be used on Android and iOS devices. Recently, Microsoft announced – in a letter sent to shareholders by Microsoft CEO Steve Ballmer – that it wants to focus on the development of "new form factors that have increasingly natural ways to use them including touch, gestures and speech". Analysing this announcement, user interface expert Bill Meisel "never expected to see mentions of natural user interfaces and machine learning in a short message to shareholders by the CEO of one of the largest companies in the U.S. Their mention as focus areas suggests that areas once viewed as leading-edge technology have achieved mainstream importance, to the degree that their successful deployment can impact the future of a major company." [43]. Meisel concludes that all three companies (Apple, Google, Microsoft) are currently "developing integrated ecosystems that can tightly couple our human intelligence with computer intelligence across a range of products. And they have the budgets to make it happen." Again, Europe has to ask itself the question if we want to leave this huge field to three US companies or if the combined expertise of our continent's language technology experts is better suited to build interactive, socially aware assistants for the speakers and users of our many different languages and cultures.

6.4.2 Novel Research Approaches and Targeted Breakthroughs

In addition to significantly improving core speech and language technologies, the development of socially aware interactive assistants requires several research breakthroughs. With regard to speech recognition, accuracy (open vocabulary, any speaker) and robustness (noise, cross-talking, distant microphones) have to be improved. Methods for self-assessment, self-adaptation, personalisation, error-recovery, learning and forgetting information, and also for moving from recognition to understanding have to be developed. Concerning speech synthesis, voices have to be made more natural and expres-

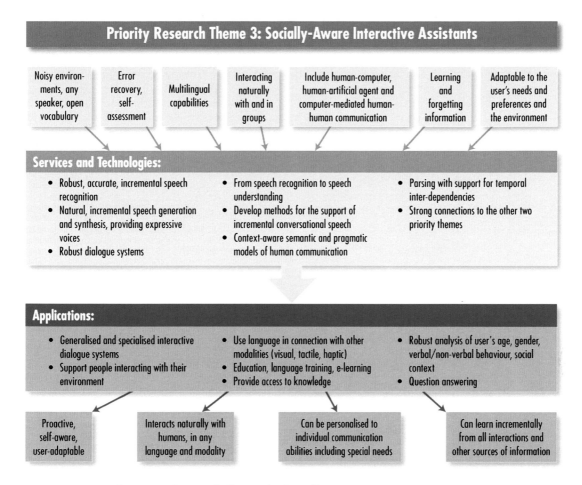

Priority Research Theme 3: Socially-Aware Interactive Assistants

Noisy environments, any speaker, open vocabulary	Error recovery, self-assessment	Multilingual capabilities	Interacting naturally with and in groups	Include human-computer, human-artificial agent and computer-mediated human-human communication	Learning and forgetting information	Adaptable to the user's needs and preferences and the environment

Services and Technologies:

- Robust, accurate, incremental speech recognition
- Natural, incremental speech generation and synthesis, providing expressive voices
- Robust dialogue systems

- From speech recognition to speech understanding
- Develop methods for the support of incremental conversational speech
- Context-aware semantic and pragmatic models of human communication

- Parsing with support for temporal inter-dependencies
- Strong connections to the other two priority themes

Applications:

- Generalised and specialised interactive dialogue systems
- Support people interacting with their environment

- Use language in connection with other modalities (visual, tactile, haptic)
- Education, language training, e-learning
- Provide access to knowledge

- Robust analysis of user's age, gender, verbal/non-verbal behaviour, social context
- Question answering

Proactive, self-aware, user-adaptable	Interacts naturally with humans, in any language and modality	Can be personalised to individual communication abilities including special needs	Can learn incrementally from all interactions and other sources of information

13: Priority Research Theme 3: Socially Aware Interactive Assistants

sive, control parameters have to be included for linguistic meaning, speaking style, emotion etc. They also have to be equipped with methods for incremental conversational speech, including filled pauses and hesitations. Likewise, speech recognition, synthesis and understanding have to be integrated, including different levels of evaluation and different levels of automated annotation.

Human communication is multimodal (including speech, facial expressions, body gestures, postures, etc.), crossmodal and fleximodal: it is based on pragmatically best suited modalities. Semantic and pragmatic models of human communication have to be developed. These have to be context-aware and model situational inter-depedencies between context and modalities for arriving at robust communication analysis (multimodal con-

tent analytics, infering knowledge from multiple sensory modalities). They have to be able to detect and recover interactively from mistakes, learning continuously and incrementally. Parsing has to model temporal inter-dependencies within and between modalities in order to maximise the assistant's human-communication-prediction ability. In order to be able to design technologies, adequate semantically and pragmatically annotated language and multimodal resources have to be produced.

A common push has to be made towards more natural dialogue. This includes, among others, the recognition and production of paralinguistics (prosody, visual cues, emotion) and a better understanding of socio-emotional functions of communicative behaviour, including group dynamics, reputation and relationship management. More natural dialogue needs more advanced dialogue models that are proactive (not only reactive), that are able to detect that recognised speech is intended as a machine command, they have to be able to interpret silence as well as direct and indirect speech acts (including lies and humour). Another prerequisite for more natural dialogue is the ability of the assistant to personalise itself to the user's preferences. The digital assistant has to operate in a transparent way and be able to participate in multi-party conversations and make use of other sensory data (GPS, RFID, cameras etc.).

There is also a strong connection to the first priority theme: the multilingual assistant should be able to do speech-to-speech translation in human-human-interaction (e. g., in meetings) and to deal with different languages, accents and dialects effectively. Systems developed should also cover at least all official languages of the EU and several regional languages.

6.4.3 Solution and Realisation

The technological and scientific state-of-the-art is at a stage that finally allows tackling the development of socially aware multilingual assistants. Progress in machine learning, including adaptation, unsupervised learning from data streams, continuous learning, and transfer learning makes it possible automatically to learn certain capabilities from data. In addition, existing language and multimodal resources enable the bootstrapping of systems. Furthermore, there is interdisciplinary progress made in, e. g., social signal processing and also knowledge representation including approaches such as the Semantic Web and Linked Open Data – especially inferences and automatic reasoning on such data sets are an important prerequisite for the technologies devised here.

Technological advances are continuously being achieved in the vision-based human behaviour analysis and synthesis fields. Ubiquitous technologies are now widely available. User-centric approaches have been largely studied and crowd-sourcing is used more and more. Quantitative and objective language technology and human-behaviour understanding technology evaluations, allowing for assessing a technological readiness level (TRL), are carried out more widely, as best practice, and language resources and publicly-available annotated recordings of human spontaneous behaviour are now available.

However, there are prohibitive factors. Technology evaluation is still limited and not conducted for all languages. There is limited availability of language resources; the necessary resources do not exist yet for all languages. Publicly-available recordings of spontaneous (rather than staged) human behaviour are sparse, especially when it comes to continuous synchronised observations of multi-party interactions. Limited progress of the technology for automatic understanding of social behaviour like rapport, empathy, envy, conflict, etc., is mainly attributed to this lack of suitable resources. In addition, we still have limited knowledge of human language and human behaviour perception processes. Automated systems often face theoretical and technological complexity of modelling and handling these processes correctly.

6.4.4 Impact

The impact of this priority theme will be wide-ranging. It will impact the work environment and processes, creativity and innovation, leisure and entertainment, and the private life. Several societal and economical facts call for, but also allow for, improved and more natural interaction between humans and the real world through machines. The ageing society requests ambient intelligence. Globalisation involves the capacity to interact in many languages, and offers a huge market for new products fully addressing this multilingual necessity.

The automation of society implies more efficiency and a 24/7 availability of services and information, while green technologies, such as advanced videoconferencing, need to be prioritised. The continuously reduced costs and

Research Priority	Phase 1: 2013-2014	Phase 2: 2015-2017	Phase 3: 2018-2020
Interacting naturally with agents	Provide usable human interface, reliable speech recognition, natural and intelligible speech synthesis, limited understanding and dialogue capabilities	Provide usable dialogue interface, context and dialogue aware speech recognition and synthesis; recognise and produce emotions, understanding capabilities, context aware dialogue, using other sensors	Provide multiparty (human-agents) interface, multiple voices, mimicking, advanced understanding and advanced personalised dialogue (indirect speech acts, incl. prosodics, lies, humor)
Using language and other modalities	Multimodal interaction (speech, facial expression, gesture, body postures)	Multimodal dialogue, fusion and fission	Fleximodal dialogue, identification of best suited modalities
Conscious of its performing capacities	Confidence in hearing/understanding, recovering from mistakes	Ability to learn continuously and incrementally from mistakes by interaction	Unsupervised learning/forgetting
Multilingual proficiency	Ensure availability or portability to major EU languages; recognise which language is spoken; multilingual access to multilingual information	More languages, accents and dialects; recognise dialects, accents; exploit limited resources; cross-lingual access to information	Speech translation in human-human interactions (multiple speakers speaking multiple languages); cross-cultural support; learn new language with small effort
Resources	Install infrastructure, benchmark data, semantically annotated data (multimodal), dialogue data	Use infrastructure, more data, more languages	Use infrastructure, more data, more languages
Evaluation	Benchmark evaluation; measures and protocols for automated speech synthesis, dialogue systems, speech translation evaluation	Measure of progress; more languages	Measure of progress; more languages

14: Priority Theme 3 – Socially-Aware Interactive Assistants: Preliminary Roadmap

speed improvement of hardware allow for affordable and better technologies, that can now easily be made available online through app stores.

At the same time we still face prohibitive factors. The cultural, political and economical dimensions of language are well perceived, but its technical dimension is not. There is still a psychological barrier for communicating with machines, although this gets more and more common through the use of smartphones and applications such as Skype or Facetime.

6.4.5 Organisation of Research

In order to improve research efficiency within a public-private partnership, the preferred infrastructure were to handle the various applications in connection with the cooperative development of technologies, including the evaluation of progress, and the production of the language and human naturalistic behaviour resources which are necessary for development and testing.

To maximise impact, it is necessary to make a substantial effort in the development of integrated systems based on open architectures, and a multilingual middleware to enable the developed functionalities to be incorporated in a wide range of software. This might best be achieved through a small number of coordinating projects, attached to a federation of strategic projects with complementary goals. These projects should be objective-driven, with clear research, technology and exploitation milestones, coordinated by an on-going road-mapping effort. This includes the production of adequate language and human naturalistic behaviour corpora, semantically annotated including prosodic and non-verbal behavioural cues. This also includes the production (acquisition and annotation) of dialogue corpora from the real world, which implies an incremental system design, and either the use of synchronised continuous observations of all involved parties, or the use of similar data available online (conversations, talk shows).

Dialogue systems evaluation still needs more research on the choice of adequate metrics and protocols. The multilingual dimension that is targeted implies the availability of language resources and language technology evaluation for all languages. Handling them all together reduces the overall effort, given the possibility to use the same best practices, tools and protocols.

6.5 CORE LANGUAGE RESOURCES AND TECHNOLOGIES

The three priority research themes share a large and heterogeneous group of core technologies for language analysis and production that provide development support through basic modules and datasets (see Figure 18, p. 68). To this group belong tools and technologies such as, among others, tokenisers, part-of-speech taggers, syntactic parsers, tools for building language models, information retrieval tools, machine learning toolkits, speech recognition and speech synthesis engines, and integrated architectures such as GATE and UIMA.

Many of these tools depend on specific datasets (i. e., language resources), for example, very large collections of linguistically annotated documents (monolingual or multilingual, aligned corpora), treebanks, grammars, lexicons, thesauri, terminologies, dictionaries, ontologies and language models. Both tools and resources can be rather general or highly task- or domain-specific, tools can be language-independent, datasets are, by definition, language-specific. As complements to the core technologies and resources there are several types of resources, such as error-annotated corpora for machine translation or spoken dialogue corpora, that are specific to one or more of the three priority themes.

A key component of this research agenda is to collect, develop and make available core technologies and resources through a shared infrastructure so that the research and technology development carried out in all themes can make use of them. Over time, this approach will improve the core technologies, as the specific research will have certain requirements on the software, extending their feature sets, performance, accuracy etc. through dynamic push-pull effetcs. Conceptualising these technologies as a set of shared core technologies will also have positive effects on their sustainability and interoperability. Also, many European languages other than English are heavily under-resourced, i. e., there are no or almost no resources or basic technologies available [12].

The European academic and industrial technology community is fully aware of the need for sharing resources such as language data (e. g., corpora), language descriptions (e. g., lexicons, thesauri, grammars), tools (e. g., taggers, stemmers, tokenisers) and core technology components (e. g., morphological, syntactic, semantic processing) as a basis for the successful development and implementation of the priority themes. Initiatives such as FLaReNet [50] and CLARIN have prepared the ground for a culture of sharing, META-NET's open resource exchange infrastructure, META-SHARE, is providing the technological platform as well as legal and organisational schemes. All language resources and basic technologies will be created under the core technologies umbrella. The effort will revolve around the following axes: Infrastructure; Coverage, Quality, Adequacy; Language Resources Acquisition; Openness; Interoperability.

6.5.1 Infrastructure

It is imperative to maintain and further to develop META-SHARE. Broad participation by the whole language technology community is essential in maintaining and extending the infrastructure so that acceptance is ensured. META-SHARE will be the key instrument to make language resources available, visible and accessible, to facilitate their sharing and exchange.

The following aspects are important for the next evolutionary steps of META-SHARE: definition of the basic data and software resources that should populate META-SHARE, multilingual coverage, the capacity to attract providers of useful resources or raw data sets, improvements in sharing mechanisms, and collaborative working practices between R&D and commercial users. There must also be a business-friendly framework to stimulate commercial use of resources, based on a sound licensing facility. Close cooperation with the three priority themes is of vital importance, especially for defining the set of needed core technologies and resources.

META-SHARE is not limited to data. Instead, it has to be seen as an international hub of resources and technologies for speech and language services from industries and communities. The development and proposal of tools and web services, including evaluation protocols and collaborative workbenches is deemed essential. The accumulation and sharing of resources and tools in a single place would lower the R&D costs for new applications in new language resource domains.

Sustainability covers preservation, accessibility, and operability (among other things). Collecting and preserving knowledge in the form of existing resources should be a key priority. A sustainability analysis must be part of a resource specification phase. Funding agencies should make a sustainability plan mandatory for projects concerned with the production of language resources.

6.5.2 Coverage, Quality, Adequacy

Innovation in LT crucially depends on language resources but currently there are not enough available resources to satisfy the needs of all languages, quantitatively and qualitatively. Language resources should be produced and made available for every language, every register, every domain to guarantee full coverage and high quality (see Figure 15). New methods of shared or distributed resource development can be exploited to achieve better coverage. It is important to assess the availability of existing resources with respect to their adequacy to applications and technology requirements. This involves assessing the maturity of the technologies for which new resources should be developed. Basic language resource kits should be supported and developed for all languages and, at least, key applications.

Automatic techniques should be promoted to guarantee quality through error detection and confidence assessment. The promotion of validation and evaluation can play a valuable role in fostering quality improvement. Evaluation should encompass technologies, resources, guidelines and documentation. But like the technologies it addresses, evaluation is constantly evolving, and new, more specific measures using innovative methodologies are needed to evaluate the reliability of language resources, while maximal use of existing tools should be ensured for the validation of resources.

Lists of basic language technologies should be compiled that should be either made available or researched and implemented for all languages covered by this agenda. These should include tools such as sentence boundary detection modules, tokenisers, lemmatisers, taggers, parsers, word/phrase aligners etc. as obligatory components for each language. These should also include resources needed for making the modules work for a given language. Other aspects are quality thresholds (minimum accuracy, speed, open availability, interoperability etc.) and cross-lingual evaluation campaigns. After partial attempts at these in the past (e. g., BLARK and ELARK, shared tasks such as CLEF, EuroMatrix Marathons, IWSLT, Morpho-Olympics etc.) a more coordinated, sustainable and also wider attempt is needed.

A Language Resources Impact Factor (LRIF) should be defined in order to enforce the practice of citation of resources on the model of scientific paper authoring and to calculate the actual research impact of resources. A reference model for creating resources will help address the current shortage of resources in terms of breadth (languages and applications) and depth (quality and volume).

In addition to the, putting it in general terms, unification of approaches mentioned above, a set of shared resources and technologies should be compiled for all the languages to be supported through the future initiative. The specifics of this shared set of dictionaries, text and speech corpora, terminologies, ontologies, lexicons, taggers etc. remain to be discussed and determined. It is important that they follow the same basic principles, cover not only general language but also several specific domains tailored to the priority themes, will be interlinked (for multilingual applications) and made available as free, public data sets for research and commercial purposes. The creation of such a shared set of base resources and technologies is imperative for the future European multilingual information society – currently there are many European languages that do not even have a corresponding corpus yet that fulfills certain requirements. National corpora only exist for a handful of languages, many of these corpora are not readily available for research purposes.

6.5.3 Language Resources Acquisition

Re-use and re-purposing should be encouraged to ensure the reuse of development methods and existing tools. With production costs constantly increasing, there is a need to invest in innovative production methods that involve automatic procedures; strategies that approach or ensure full automation for high-quality resource production should be promoted. It is worth considering the power of social media to build resources, especially for those languages where no language resources built by experts exist yet.

There are several promising experiments in crowd-sourcing data collection tasks. Crowd-sourcing makes it possible to mobilise large groups of human talent around the world with just the right language skills so that we can collect what we need when we need it. For instance, it has been estimated that Mechanical Turk translation is 10 to 60 times less expensive than professional translation. A particularly sensitive case is that of less-resourced languages, where language technology should be developed rapidly to help minority-language speakers access education and the Information Society [51, 19, 20, 21].

6.5.4 Openness

There is a strong trend towards open data, i. e., data that are easily obtainable and that can be used with few, if any, restrictions. Sharing data and tools has become a viable solution towards encouraging open data [52], and the community is strongly investing in facilities such as META-SHARE for the discovery and use of resources. These facilities could represent an optimal intermediate solution to respond to the needs for data variety, ease of retrieval, better data description and community-wide access, while at the same time assisting in clearing the intricate issues associated with intellectual property rights (see Section 6.7 for more details).

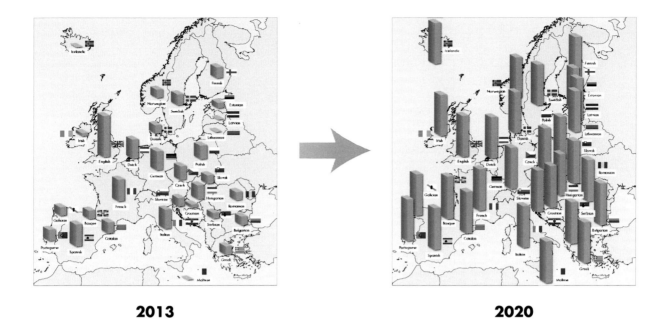

2013 → **2020**

15: Towards appropriate and adequate coverage of language resources and technologies for Europe

6.5.5 Interoperability

Interoperability of resources seeks to maximise the extent to which they are compatible and therefore integratable at various levels, so as to allow, for instance, the merging of data or tools coming from different sources. All stakeholders need to join forces to drive forward the use of existing and emerging standards, at least in the areas where there is some degree of consensus.

6.5.6 Organisation of Research

In order to optimise the efficiency of shared core technologies for language analysis and production as well as the further development of the infrastructure, maximise the infrastructure's impact, and ensure that requirements for research and development are met at the necessary depth for all languages in all priority themes, the organisation of this shared agenda theme should adopt the following principles: It is necessary to invest in the further development of an integrated infrastructure (i. e., META-SHARE) based on an open architecture, enabling the sharing and further development of resources. The infrastructure should support technology-specific challenges and shared tasks in order to accelerate innovation breakthrough and market-readiness for desperately needed technologies. Concerted activities and policies facilitating the sharing of resources overcoming all stumbling blocks on the way to technical, organisational and legal interoperability should be supported. EU level research must be aligned and tightly coordinated with efforts on the national levels, so that coverage and language-specific developments are efficiently achieved. An important aspect of this coordination effort is concerned with the META-NET White Paper Series [12]: in the 30 different white papers we have concrete and specific assessments of the language- and country-specific situation with regard to demands and technology gaps. The next step is to address and to fill these gaps with high-quality and robust core technologies and language resources.

Research Priority	Phase 1: 2013-2014	Phases 2 and 3: 2015-2020
Infrastructure	Maintain and extend facility(-ies) for sharing resource data and tools; promote accurate and reliable documentation of resources through metadata; cooperation between infrastructure initiatives to avoid the duplication of effort	Automatically accumulate descriptions and resources; multilingual coverage, ease of conversion into uniform formats; integrate web services (SaaS)
Coverage, quality, adequacy	Increase number of resources to address LT and application needs; address formal and content quality by promoting evaluation and validation; promote evaluation and validation activities and the dissemination of their outcomes	Increase number of resources to address LT and application needs; provide HQ resources for all European languages
Acquisition	Define and disseminate LR production best practices; enforce reusing and repurposing; towards the full automation of LR data production; methods for collaborative creation and extension of HQ resources, also to increase coverage; implement workflows of language processing services for acquisition of resources required for the implementation of the priority themes; bridge acquisition methods with linked open data and big data; share the effort for production of LRs between international bodies and individual countries	
Openness	Educate key players with basic legal know-how; elaborate specific, simple and harmonised licensing solutions for data resources; promote copyright exception for research purposes; develop legal and technical solutions for privacy protection; opt for openness of resources, especially publicly funded ones; ensure that publicly funded resources are publicly available free of charge; clear IPR at the early stages of production; try to ensure that re-use is permitted	
Interoperability	Standardisation activities, make standards operational and put them in use; establish permanent Standards Watch; promote and disseminate standards to students and young researchers; encourage/enforce use of best practices or standards in production projects; identify new mature areas for standardisation and promote joint efforts between R&D and industry	

16: Core language resources and technologies: Preliminary Roadmap

6.6 A EUROPEAN SERVICE PLATFORM FOR LANGUAGE TECHNOLOGIES

We argue for and recommend the design and implementation of an ambitious large-scale platform as a central motor for research and innovation in the next phase of IT evolution and as a ubiquitous resource for the multilingual European society. The platform will be used for testing, show casing, proof-of-concept demonstration, avant-garde adoption, experimental and operational service composition, and fast and economical service delivery to enterprises and end-users (see Figure 17).

The proposed creation of a powerful cloud or sky computing platform (see Section 3.5) for a wide range of services dealing with human language, knowledge and emotion will not only benefit the individual and corporate users of these technologies but also the providers. Large-scale ICT infrastructures and innovation clusters such as this suggested platform are also foreseen in the Digital Agenda for Europe (see [5], p. 24).

Users will be able to receive customised integrated services without having to install, combine, support and maintain the software. They will have access to specialised solutions even if they do not use these regularly.

Language technology providers will have ample opportunity to offer stand-alone or integrated services.

Providers of language services rendered by human language professionals will be able to use the platform for enhancing their services by means of appropriate technology and for providing their services stand-alone or integrated into other application services.

Researchers will have a virtual laboratory for testing, combining, and benchmarking their technologies and for exposing them in realistic trials to real tasks and users.

Providers of services that can be enabled or enhanced by text and speech processing will utilise the platform for testing the needed LT functionalities and for integrating them into their own solutions.

Citizens and corporate users will enjoy the benefits of language technology early and at no or reasonable costs through a large variety of generic and specialised services offered at a single source.

In order to allow for the gigantic range of foreseeable and currently not yet foreseeable solutions, the infrastructure will have to host all relevant simple services, including components, tools and data resources, as well as various layers or components of higher services that incorporate simpler ones. META-SHARE can play an important role in the design of the platform (see Section 6.5).

A top layer consists of **language processing** such as text filters, tokenisation, spell, grammar and style checking, hyphenation, lemmatising and parsing. At a slightly deeper level, services will be offered that realise some degree and form of **language understanding** including entity and event extraction, opinion mining and translation. Both basic language processing and understanding will be used by services that support **human communication** or realise human-machine interaction. Part of this layer are question answering and dialogue systems as well as email response applications. Another component will bring in services for processing and storing **knowledge** gained by and used for understanding and communication. This part will include repositories of linked data and ontologies, as well as services for building, using and maintaining them. These in turn permit a certain range of rational capabilities often attributed to a notion of intelligence. The goal is not to model the entire human intelligence

but rather to realise selected forms of **inference** that are needed for utilising and extending knowledge, for understanding and for successful communication. These forms of inference permit better decision support, pro-active planning and autonomous adaptation. A final part of services will be dedicated to **human emotion**. Since people are largely guided by their emotions and strongly affected by the emotions of others, truly user-centred IT need facilities for detecting and interpreting emotion and even for expressing emotional states in communication.

We consider the paradigm of federated cloud services or sky computing with its emerging standards such as OCCI, OVM and CDMI and toolkits such a OpenNebula as the appropriate approach for realising the ambitious infrastructure. All three priority areas of this SRA will be able to contribute to and at the same time draw immense benefits from this platform. There are strong reasons for aiming at a single service platform for the three areas and for the different types of technologies. They share many basic components and they need to be combined for many valuable applications, including the selected showcase solutions of the three areas.

Implementation of the Platform

The creation of this platform has to be supported by public funding. Because of the high requirements concerning performance, reliability, user support, scalability, persistence as well as data protection and conformance with privacy regulation, the platform needs to be established by a consortium with strong commercial partners and also be operated by this consortium or a commercial contractor. A similar platform with slightly different desiderata and functionalities is currently built under the name Helix-Nebula for the Earth Sciences with the help of the following commercial partners: Atos, Capgemini, CloudSigma, Interoute, Logica, Orange Business Services, SAP, SixSq, Telefonica, Terradue, Thales, The Server Labs and T-Systems. Partners are also the Cloud

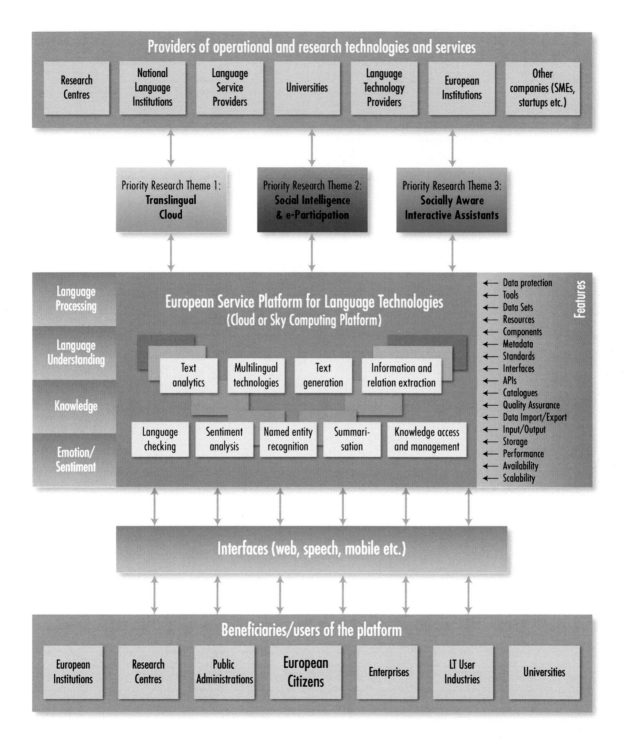

17: European Service Platform for Language Technologies

Security Alliance, the OpenNebula Project and the European Grid Infrastructure. These are working together with major research centres in the Earth Sciences to establish the targeted federated and secure high-performance computing cloud platform.

The intended platform for LT and neighbouring fields would be intended for a mix of commercial and non-commercial services. It would be cost-free for all providers of non-commercial services (cost-free and advertisement-free) including research systems, experimental services and freely shared resources but it would raise revenues by charging a proportional commission on all commercially provided services. In order to reduce dependence on individual companies and software products, the base technology should be supplied by open toolkits and standards such as OpenNebula and OCCI.

For each priority research theme, chances for successful showcasing and successful commercial innovation will increase tremendously if usable services of required strength and reliability could be offered on such a platform.

The platform will considerably lower the barrier for market entry for innovative technologies, especially for products and services offered by SMEs. Still, these stakeholders may not have the resources, expertise, and time to create the necessary interfaces to integrate their results into real-life services, let alone the overarching platform itself. There is still a gap between research prototypes and products that have been engineered and tested for robust applications. Moreover, many innovative developments require access to special kinds of language resources such as recordings of spoken commands to smartphones, which are difficult to get for several reasons.

Thus the service platform will be an important instrument for supporting the entire innovation chain, but, in addition, interoperability standards, interfacing tools, middle-ware, and reference service architectures need to be developed and constantly adapted. Many of these may not be generic enough to serve all application areas, so

that much of the work in resource and service integration will have to take place in the respective priority theme research actions.

6.7 LEGAL CHALLENGES

Legal challenges are involved on multiple levels in our future research and technology plans as described in this agenda. One of the key challenges for our community and also for the policy makers is to push for the development of a common legal framework that would facilitate resource sharing efforts abiding by the law, benefiting from the adoption of "fair use" principles and appropriate copyright exceptions. It is of utmost importance that legislation regarding resource use and resource acquisition be harmonised, and even standardised, for all types of language resources, and that free use be allowed, at least for research or non-profit purposes (see Section 6.5).

Other areas in which we are facing or in which we expect legal challenges are the "trust" features of the European Language Technology Platform, which needs to exhibit a maximum level of data security in order to protect confidential documents (from contracts to patient data), or novel methods of acquiring written or spoken data for language resources. Any grant of access to language resources should ideally include not only the right to read the relevant content but also to allow transformative uses, dissemination and distribution of such resources and their derivatives, according to the needs and policies of language resources owners and users. Not only the acquisition but also the sharing and distribution of language resources is constantly hindered or completely disabled by legal aspects which should ideally be resolved once and for all. Legal issues such as these are severe stumbling blocks that can bring innovation to a complete standstill. In addition, content or approaches to data privacy or security that are legal in one country may be illegal in another. These aspects can be partially addressed on the software level (for example, through appropriate metadata records that reflect different legal realms) but should ideally be harmonised on the European or global level. META-NET favours and aligns itself with the growing open data and open source movement and the idea of opening up data, resources and technologies (especially those whose development was supported through public funding) instead of locking them away. META-NET advocates the use of a model licensing scheme with a firm orientation towards the creation of an openness culture and the relevant ecosystem for language resources.

6.8 LANGUAGES TO BE SUPPORTED

The research and technology development programme specified in this agenda has a much broader scope in terms of languages to be supported than our study "Europe's Languages in the Digital Age" (Section 4, p. 27 ff.). The set of languages to be reflected with corresponding technologies include not only the currently 23 official languages of the European Union but also recognised and unrecognised regional languages and the languages of associated countries or non-member states. Equally important are the minority and immigrant languages that are in active use by a significant population in Europe (for Germany, these are, among others, Turkish and Russian; for the UK, these include Bengali, Urdu/Hindi and Punjabi). An important set of languages outside our continent are those of important political and trade partners such as, for example, Chinese, Indonesian, Japanese, Korean, Russian, and Thai. META-NET already has good working relationships with several of the respective official bodies, especially EFNIL (European Federation of National Institutions for Language), NPLD (Network to Promote Linguistic Diversity, [51]), and also the Maaya World Network for Linguistic Diversity.

The concrete composition of languages to be supported by this agenda's research programme up until the year 2020 and beyond, depends on the concrete composition of participating countries and regions and also on the specific nature of the funding instruments used and combined for realising the ambituous plan. It remains to be discussed what it means for a language to be supported through this strategic programme; most probably, the level of support will have to be determined through a concrete set of specific resources and specific base technologies that need to be researched and developed for a given language and that need to fulfill certain requirements (with regard to, among others, coverage, precision, quality, speed etc.). The next level of support would, then, be determined by including a language in one or more of the priority research themes.

Not all countries have the required expertise or human resources to take care of the technology support for their languages. For example, in Iceland there is not a single position in LT at any Icelandic university or college and there is only one company that works in this area. Those colleagues who work on LT at universities and research institutes come from either language or computer science departments; their main duties are not related to LT, still they managed to produce a few basic technologies and resources but advanced types of resources do not exist at all for Icelandic, nor do they for many other under-resourced languages. This is why we need to intensify research and establish techniques, methods and instruments for research and knowledge transfer so that colleagues in countries such as Iceland can benefit as much as possible for their own language from the research carried out in other countries for other languages. Bootstrapping the set of core language technologies and resources for all languages spoken in Europe is not a matter of a few countries joining forces but a challenge on the European scale that must be addressed accordingly to avoid digital exclusion and secure future business development.

META-NET realises that Europe is a multi-ethnic region in which many more languages than only the official ones are spoken. Therefore, it is important not only to carry out research and technology development on the official and a few additional languages but also to work on those languages that are in active use by a significant part of the population, in order to address the severe issue of linguistic ghettoisation and finally to bring about a truly multilingual European information society.

As regards funding the programme we suggest an approach that involves multiple stakeholders, especially the European Union, the Member States, Associated Countries, other countries and also regions, not only in Europe but ultimately also on other continents. Research on advanced, sophisticated monolingual technologies is to be supported by the respective countries' funding agencies primarily. Research on multilingual technologies and also research on basic technologies and resources for under-resourced languages needs to be supported by the EU along with the respective countries and regions. Specific procedures for research and knowledge transfer need to be agreed upon and put into action so that the speakers of these languages can benefit from our activities as much and as quickly as possible. In order to provide basic technology support for those languages spoken in Europe with active hubs of research outside our continent, connections to the leading research centres need to be established or intensified so that Europe can benefit from technologies that have been developed by these centres. If technologies exist, funding schemes need to be established so that they can be adopted, if necessary, to the standards that will be put into practice in Europe in the years to come, especially with regard to sharing, distribution, data formats, APIs and inclusion in the European Language Technology Platform.

6.9 RESEARCH ORGANISATION

The three proposed priority research themes overlap in technologies and challenges – this is intended. The overlap reflects the coherence and maturation of the field. At the same time, the resulting division of labour and sharing of resources and results is a precondition for the realisation of this highly ambitious programme.

All three themes need to benefit from progress in core technologies of language analysis and production such as morphological, syntactic and semantic parsing and generation. But each of the three areas will concentrate on one central area of language technology: the Translingual Cloud will focus on cross-lingual technologies such as translation and interpretation; the Social Intelligence strand will take care of knowledge discovery, text analytics and related technologies; the research dedicated to the Interactive Assistants will take on technologies such as speech and multimodal interfaces (see Figure 18).

Except for a few large national projects and programmes such as Technolangue and Quaero in France, Verbmobil and Theseus in Germany and DARPA Communicator and GALE in the US, the field of language technology does not have experience with research efforts of the magnitude and scope required for the targeted advances and plans in this SRA. Nevertheless, our technology area has to follow developments in other key engineering disciplines and speed up technology evolution by massive collaboration based on competitive division of labour and sharing of resources and results. In our reflection on optimal schemes for organising we tried to draw lessons from our own field's recent history and to capitalise on experience from other fields by adopting approaches that proved successful and evading encountered pitfalls.

The final model for the organisation of collaboration will have to be guided by a thoughtful combination of the following basic approaches.

Flexible collaborative approach: For each priority theme, one or several very large cooperating and competing lead projects will share an infrastructure for evaluation, communication and resources (data and base technologies). Mechanisms for reducing or terminating partner involvements and for adding new partners or subcon-

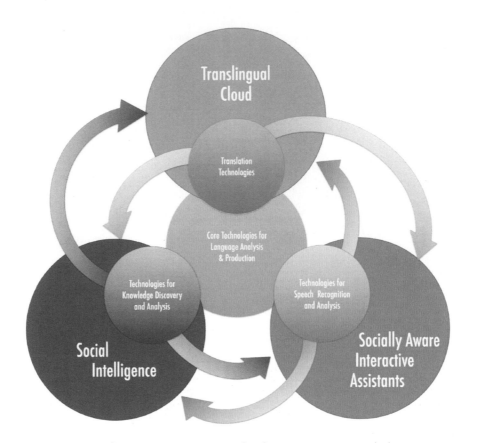

18: Scientific cooperation among the three priority research themes

tracted contributors should provide flexibility. A number of smaller projects including national and regional projects will provide building blocks for particular languages, tasks, component technologies or resources. A cooperation scheme will be designed for effectively and flexibly involving EC-funding, contributions from member states, industrial associations, and language communities, among others [53]. The choice of funding instruments will be determined in due time.

Staged approach: Two major phases are foreseen (2015-2017, 2018-2020). The major phases should be synchronised among the themes and also projects.

Evolutionary approach: Instead of banking on one selected paradigm, competing approaches will be followed in parallel with shared schemes for evaluation, merging, adopting and discontinuing research threads so that the two elements of successful evolutionary research approaches, selection and cross-fertilisation, are exploited to the maximum extent possible.

Analytical approach: Instead of the currently predominant search for an ideal one-fits-all approach, the research will focus on observed quality barriers and not shun computationally expensive dedicated solutions for overcoming particular obstacles.

Bootstrapping approach: Better systems can be derived from more and better data and through new insights. In turn, improved systems can be used to gain better data and new insights. Thus the combination of the analytical evolutionary approach with powerful machine learning techniques will be the basis for a technology bootstrapping, which has been the by far most fruitful scheme for the development of highly complex technologies.

Close cooperation with relevant areas of service and technology industries: In order to increase chances of successful commercialisation and to obtain convincing and sufficiently tested demonstrations of novel applications, the relevant industrial sectors must be strongly integrated into the entire research cycle.

Tighter research-innovation cycle: Through the collaboration between research, commercial services and commercial technology industries, especially through the shared evaluation metrics and continuous testing, the usual push-model of technology transfer will hopefully be substituted by a pull-model, in which commercial technology users can ask for specific solutions. In the envisaged research scheme, incentives will be created for competing teams each composed of researchers, commercial users and commercial developers by the participating enterprises for initiating successful innovations.

Interdisciplinary approach: A number of science, technology and service areas need to be integrated into the research from day one. Some technology areas such as speech technologies, language checking and authoring systems need to be represented by providers of state-of-the-art commercial products.

The coordination among the three research strands poses administrative challenges. Because of the described interdependencies and also because of the need to maintain and improve the obtained level of cohesion and community spirit in the European Language Technology community, a coordinating body is needed. Whether such an entity is jointly carried by the three areas or by a separate support project, needs to be determined in the upcoming discussion on the appropriate support instruments for the identified research priorities.

6.10 SUPPORTIVE POLICY MAKING

Technological progress would be even more efficient and effective if the proposed research effort could be accompanied by appropriate supportive policy making in several areas. One of these areas is multilingualism. Overcoming language barriers can greatly influence the future of the EU and the whole planet [19, 20, 21]. Solutions for better communication and for access to content in the native languages of the users would reaffirm the role of the EC to serve the needs of the EU citizens. A substantial connection to the infrastructural program CEF could help to speed up the transfer of research results to badly needed services for the European economy and public. At the same time, use cases should cover areas where the European societal needs massively overlap with business opportunities to achieve funding investment that pays back, ideally public-private partnerships.

Language policies supporting multilingualism can create a tangible boost for technology development. Some of the best results in machine translation have been achieved in Catalonia, where legislation supporting the use of the Catalan language has created an increased demand for automatic translation.

Numerous US-originating breakthroughs in IT that have subsequently led to commercially successful products of great economic impact could only be achieved by a combination of systematic long-term research support coupled with public procurement. Many types of aircraft or the autonomous land vehicle would not have seen the light of the day without massive military support, even the internet or the speech technology behind Apple Siri heavily benefited from sequences of DARPA programmes often followed by government contracts procuring earlier versions of the technology for military or civilian use by the public sector.

The greed for originality on the side of the public research funding bodies and their constant trial-and-error search for new themes that might finally help the European IT sector to be in time with their innovations has often caused the premature abortion of promising developments, whose preliminary results were more than once taken up by research centres and enterprises in the US. An example in language technology is the progress in statistical machine translation. Much of the groundwork laid in the German government-sponsored project Verbmobil (1993–2000) was later taken up by DARPA research and industrial systems including Google Translate.

In order to drive technology evolution with public funding to a stage of maturity where first sample solutions can deliver visible benefits to the European citizens and where the private sector can take up technologies to then develop a wide range of more sophisticated profitable applications, we strongly advocate a combination of

1. language policies supporting the status of European languages in the public sector,

2. long-term systematic research efforts with the goal to realise badly needed pre-competitive basic services,

3. procurement of solution development by European public administrations.

European policy making should also speed up technology evolution by helping the research community to gain affordable and less restrictive access to text and speech data repositories, especially to data that have been collected with public support for scientific and cultural purposes. Today, outdated legislation and restrictive interpretation of existing law hinder the effective use of many valuable data collections such as, for example, several so-called national corpora. The research community urgently needs the help of European and national policy makers for modes of use of these data that would boost technology development without infringing on the economic interests of authors and publishers.

TOWARDS A SHARED EUROPEAN PROGRAMME FOR MULTILINGUAL EUROPE 2020: NEXT STEPS

7.1 SUMMARY

In this Strategic Research Agenda META-NET recommends setting up a large, multi-year programme on language technologics to build the technological foundations for a truly multilingual Europe. We suggest to concentrate future efforts in this field on three priority research themes: Translingual Cloud; Social Intelligence and e-Participation; Socially-Aware Interactive Assistants. We also suggest to concentrate on two additional themes. On the one hand there is the overarching issue of researching and further developing core language resources and base technologies that are needed by the three priority themes and that, for many of Europe's languages, do not exist yet. On the other, we recommend to design and to implement the European Language Technology Platform as a means to collect and to offer all language technology-related applications and services, designed and built in Europe for the European citizen.

The research strands and associated sets of applications we suggest to build in the next ten years are of utmost importance for Europe. Through these technologies we will be able to overcome language barriers in spoken and written communication, we will be able to carry out country- and language-border-crossing debates and we will enable new forms and means of communication. We are confident that the impact of our technologies will be so immense that they will be able to help establishing a sense of a European identity in the majority of European citizens. The research plan described in this agenda will generate a countless number of opportunities, it will significantly participate to Europe's future growth and will secure Europe's position in many global markets.

7.2 SPECIFIC ROADMAPS

The roadmaps presented in this Strategic Research Agenda provide indicative information as regards the actual research lines and phases within the priority themes. The roadmaps show the current state of discussion within META-NET and our recommendations how to move forward. Upcoming EC-funded projects will continue work on the roadmaps, preparing more detailed and more concrete phases. The project QTLaunchPad, which started in June 2012 and which puts an emphasis on quality translation, is taking care of pushing forward the roadmap for the Translingual Cloud priority theme (Section 6.2). It is expected that two or three additional projects which will be funded under the final FP7 call, starting in late 2013, will take care of the roadmaps for the two other priority themes (Sections 6.3 and 6.4) and most likely also the European Language Technology Platform (Section 6.6). Only when more details are known with regard to the available research steps and interdependencies and also the potential funding instruments can our plans and the shared programme be specified in a more detailed way. For the field of language technology the scope of the shared programme is unprecedented: we recommend to set up a ten-year programme in a total of five areas, involving the European Union and additional countries.

G. Rehm and H. Uszkoreit (eds.), *META-NET Strategic Research Agenda for Multilingual Europe 2020*, White Paper Series, DOI: 10.1007/978-3-642-36349-8_7, © The Author(s) 2013

7.3 TOWARDS A SHARED EUROPEAN PROGRAMME

The plans foreseen in this SRA can be successfully realised and implemented using several different measures and instruments, for example, through clusters of projects or a certain number of coordinated projects. Due to the scope and duration of the suggested action, our preferred option is to set up a shared programme between the European Commission and the Member States as well as Associated Countries. First steps along those lines have been taken at META-NET's META-FORUM 2012 conference in Brussels, Belgium, on June 21, 2012, when representatives of several European funding agencies (Bulgaria, Czech Republic, France, Hungary, The Netherlands, Slovenia) who participated in a panel discussion on this topic, unanimously expressed the urgent need for setting up such a shared programme [54].

A sizable portion of the research proposed in this SRA under the umbrella of the three priority themes is to be carried out in the Horizon 2020 programme. The European service platform for language technologies is a very good fit for the Connecting Europe Facility programme (CEF) while large parts of the core technologies for language analysis and production, especially monolingual base resources and technologies, are good candidates for support through national and regional programmes (see Section 6.8). Furthermore, it is important to include the technological needs and innovative ideas of Europe's SMEs, bigger companies and the startup scene in the further shaping of the shared programme.

The shared programme will include a carefully planned governance structure. First steps towards establishing a structure have already been taken within META-NET. The network of excellence has an Executive Board with currently 12 members, the operations of the network and its bodies are specified in the META-NET Statutes [55]. Furthermore, a legal person for the META-NET network was established. This legal person, META-TRUST AISBL, is an international non-profit organisation under Belgian law [56]. These proven and established structures can be used as starting points for the governance structure of the future programme but we are open to any suggestions for modifications, especially as the final governance structure will also be partially determined by the concrete funding instruments to be used for establishing the programme. The main responsibilities of the governance structure will be to perform checks, to monitor and to evaluate progress and to maintain and to modify the strategic agenda and roadmaps. All major research strands and paths specified in the roadmaps will be complemented with evaluation campaigns that set quality levels for the implemented technologies. These evaluation campaigns will act as major quality assurance instruments so that the research and development results comply with industry expectations and performance standards.

There are several options how to organise the research proposed in this strategic agenda. In June 2012 we have started discussing two possible instruments within META-NET that mainly aim at establishing a shared European programme – other options still have to be screened; new options might emerge from the Horizon 2020 and CEF programmes. The two candidate instruments are an Article 185 Initiative (see Section 7.3.1) and a Contractual Public-Private Partnership (PPP, see Section 7.3.2).

7.3.1 Article 185 Initiative

To quote Article 185 of the Treaty of the Functioning of the European Union (TFEU): "In implementing the multiannual framework programme, the Union may make provision, in agreement with the Member States concerned, for participation in research and development programmes undertaken by several Member States [...]." Currently there are four joint programmes running as Article 185 Initiatives [57]: Ambient Assisted Living (AAL), Baltic Sea research (Bonus), a programme in the field of metrology (EMRP) and a programme for research performing SMEs and their partners (Eurostars).

A key idea behind Article 185 is to coordinate national programmes in order to reduce the fragmentation of research efforts carried out on the national or regional level. Among the goals to be achieved are to reach critical mass in certain research areas, to ensure better use of scarce resources and to find common answers and approaches to common needs and interests. Member states are given the opportunity to exchange good practice, to avoid unnecessary overlaps of efforts, to exchange information and expertise and to learn from each other.

The Seventh Framework Programme states that an Article 185 Initiative can be launched in areas to be identified in close association with the Member States on the basis of a series of criteria: relevance to EU objectives; the clear definition of the objective to be pursued and its relevance to the objectives of the Framework Programme; presence of a pre-existing basis (existing or envisaged research programmes); European added value; critical mass, with regard to the size and the number of programmes involved and the similarity of activities they cover; efficiency of Article 185 as the most appropriate means for achieving the objectives. Each Article 185 Initiative is set up individually through a decision of the European Parliament and of the European Council, following a proposal from the European Commission. The implementation requires the establishment or existence of a legal Dedicated Implementation Structure (DIS) which should exist before the Council's decision. The DIS takes care of programme management and calls for proposals, selection of projects and follow-ups and financial management.

7.3.2 Contractual Public-Private Partnership

While many details of the upcoming programme Horizon 2020 are still under discussion, Contractual PPPs are currently emerging as the primary model to implement parts of the programme objectives with regard to sizeable, roadmap-based research and innovation efforts within the technology pillar of H2020, drawing also on resources beyond the EU support and related matching funds. The EC's proposal for Horizon 2020 states that "greater impact should also be achieved by combining Horizon 2020 and private sector funds within public-private partnerships in key areas where research and innovation could contribute to Europe's wider competitiveness goals and help tackle societal challenges" [58]. PPPs are an important mechanism for focusing research and innovation, ensuring stakeholders engagement and, above all, for improving the impact of EU support on Europe's competitiveness, growth and jobs creation (see [5], p. 24). A public-private partnership is defined as "a partnership where private sector partners, the Union and, where appropriate, other partners, commit to jointly support the development and implementation of a research and innovation programme or activities". Similar instruments are JTIs (Joint Technology Initiatives), ETPs (European Technology Platforms) and institutional PPPs which are a counterpart to Contractual PPPs.

For Contractual PPPs, a Contractual Agreement is foreseen between the EC and private and public partners that specifies the objectives of the partnership, commitments of the partners, target outputs and the activities that require support from Horizon 2020. PPPs are to be identified in an open and transparent way based on all of the following criteria: the added value of action at Union level; the scale of impact on industrial competitiveness, sustainable growth and socio-economic issues; the long-term commitment from all partners based on a shared vision and clearly defined objectives; the scale of the resources involved and the ability to leverage additional investments in research and innovation; a clear definition of roles for each of the partners and agreed key performance indicators over the period chosen (see [58], p. 21).

Setting up a contractual PPP does not require a decision in the European Parliament.

7.4 CONCLUSIONS

The research plans specified in this SRA are, among others, a good match for an Article 185 Initiative and also for a Contractual PPP. It remains to be discussed which instrument is considered the most appropriate one to realise and implement the three priority research themes, the set of core technologies and shared resources and also the European service platform for language technology. Due to the scope, size and duration of the shared programme, a combination of instruments could also be a promising avenue, for example, to fund the actual research to be carried out in the three priority themes through Horizon 2020 and to concentrate on CEF concerning the development of the European Language Technology Platform.

REFERENCES

[1] Daniel Jurafsky and James H. Martin. *Speech and Language Processing (Maschinelle Verarbeitung gesprochener und geschriebener Sprache)*. Prentice Hall, 2nd edition, 2009.

[2] Christopher D. Manning and Hinrich Schütze. *Foundations of Statistical Natural Language Processing (Grundlagen der statistischen Sprachverarbeitung)*. MIT Press, 1999.

[3] Language Technology World (LT World). http://www.lt-world.org.

[4] Ronald Cole, Joseph Mariani, Hans Uszkoreit, Giovanni Battista Varile, Annie Zaenen, and Antonio Zampolli, editors. *Survey of the State of the Art in Human Language Technology (Sprachtechnologie: Überblick über den Stand der Kunst)*. Cambridge University Press, 1998.

[5] European Commission. A Digital Agenda for Europe, 2010. http://ec.europa.eu/information_society/digital-agenda/publications/.

[6] European Commission. Multilingualism: an Asset for Europe and a Shared Commitment, 2008. http://ec.europa.eu/languages/pdf/comm2008_en.pdf.

[7] The Council of the European Union. Council Resolution of 21 November 2008 on a European strategy for multilingualism, November 2008. http://eur-lex.europa.eu/LexUriServ/LexUriServ.do?uri=OJ:C:2008:320:0001:01:en:HTML.

[8] Economist Intelligence Unit The Economist. Competing across borders. how cultural and communication barriers affect business, 2012. http://www.managementthinking.eiu.com/competing-across-borders.html.

[9] European Commission. Languages, 2012. http://ec.europa.eu/languages/.

[10] The Language Rich Europe Consortium. *Towards a Language Rich Europe. Multilingual Essays on Language Policies and Practices*. British Council, July 2011. http://www.language-rich.eu/fileadmin/content/pdf/LRE_FINAL_WEB.pdf.

[11] Special Eurobarometer 386/77.1. Europeans and their Languages, June 2012. http://ec.europa.eu/languages/languages-of-europe/eurobarometer-survey_en.htm.

[12] Georg Rehm and Hans Uszkoreit, editors. *META-NET White Paper Series: Europe's Languages in the Digital Age*. Springer, Heidelberg, New York, Dordrecht, London, 2012. This series comprises 31 volumes on the following 30 European languages: Basque, Bulgarian, Catalan, Croatian, Czech, Danish, Dutch, English, Estonian, Finnish, French, Galician, German, Greek, Hungarian, Icelandic, Irish, Italian, Latvian, Lithuanian, Maltese, Norwegian (available in Bokmål and Nynorsk), Polish, Portuguese, Romanian, Serbian, Slovak, Slovene, Spanish, Swedish. http://www.meta-net.eu/whitepapers.

[13] Gianni Lazzari. Human Language Technologies for Europe, 2006. http://cordis.europa.eu/documents/documentlibrary/90834371EN6.pdf.

[14] Andrew Joscelyne and Rose Lockwood. The EUROMAP Study. Benchmarking HLT progress in Europe, 2003. http://cst.dk/dandokcenter/FINAL_Euromap_rapport.pdf.

[15] European Commission. Connecting Europe Facility: Commission adopts plan for €50 billion boost to European networks, 2011. http://europa.eu/rapid/pressReleasesAction.do?reference=IP/11/1200.

[16] European Commission. Horizon 2020: The Framework Programme for Research and Innovation, 2012. http://ec.europa.eu/research/horizon2020/.

G. Rehm and H. Uszkoreit (eds.), *META-NET Strategic Research Agenda for Multilingual Europe 2020*, White Paper Series, DOI: 10.1007/978-3-642-36349-8, © The Author(s) 2013

[17] Reinhilde Veugelers. New ICT Sectors: Platforms for European Growth?, August 2012. Issue 2012/14. http://www.bruegel.org/publications/.

[18] Directorate-General of the UNESCO. Intersectoral Mid-term Strategy on Languages and Multilingualism, 2007. http://unesdoc.unesco.org/images/0015/001503/150335e.pdf.

[19] Laurent Vannini and Hervé Le Crosnier, editors. *Net.Lang – Towards the Multilingual Cyberspace*. C&F éditions, Paris, March 2012. The Maaya World Network for Linguistic Diversity. http://net-lang.net.

[20] UNESCO Information for All Programme. International Conference Linguistic and Cultural Diversity in Cyberspace: Final Document. Lena Resolution, July 2008. http://portal.unesco.org/pv_obj_cache/pv_obj_id_0119EB89EE87D73C0BE7BAD0BFC267E5DD760000/filename/lena_resolution_en.pdf.

[21] UNESCO Information for All Programme. Second International Conference Linguistic and Cultural Diversity in Cyberspace: Final Document. Yakutsk Call for Action, July 2011. http://www.maayajo.org/IMG/pdf/Call_for_action_Yakutsk_EN-2.pdf.

[22] Directorate-General Information Society & Media of the European Commission. User Language Preferences Online, 2011. http://ec.europa.eu/public_opinion/flash/fl_313_en.pdf.

[23] Daniel Ford and Josh Batson. Languages of the World (Wide Web), July 2011. http://googleresearch.blogspot.com/2011/07/languages-of-world-wide-web.html.

[24] Conrad Quilty-Harper. Chinese internet users to overtake English language users by 2015, September 2012. http://www.telegraph.co.uk/technology/broadband/9567934/Chinese-internet-users-to-overtake-English-language-users-by-2015.html.

[25] Eric Fisher. Language communities of Twitter (European detail), October 2011. http://www.flickr.com/photos/walkingsf/6276642489/. Licensed under Creative Commons Attribution 2.0 Generic (CC BY 2.0).

[26] Directorate-General for Translation of the European Commission. Size of the Language Industry in the EU, 2009. http://ec.europa.eu/dgs/translation/publications/studies.

[27] European Commission. Languages mean business, 2011. http://ec.europa.eu/languages/languages-mean-business/.

[28] Global Industry Analysts. Spech Technology: A Global Strategic Business Report, March 2012. http://www.strategyr.com/Speech_Technology_Market_Report.asp.

[29] Donald A. DePalma and Nataly Kelly. The Business Case for Machine Translation. How Organizations Justify and Adopt Automated Translation, August 2009. Common Sense Advisory. http://www.commonsenseadvisory.com/AbstractView.aspx?ArticleID=859.

[30] Franz Och. Breaking down the language barrier – six years in, April 2012. http://googleblog.blogspot.de/2012/04/breaking-down-language-barriersix-years.html.

[31] Mark Vanderbeeken. The English Language Innovation Bias, 2012. http://www.wired.com/beyond_the_beyond/2012/06/mark-vanderbeeken-the-english-language-innovation-bias/.

[32] P. Nikiforos Diamandouros. Ombudsman criticises Commission's restrictive language policy for public consultations. Press release no. 17/2012, October 2012. http://www.ombudsman.europa.eu/el/press/release.faces/en/12029/html.bookmark.

[33] European Commission. Report on cross-border e-commerce in the EU, 2009. http://ec.europa.eu/consumers/strategy/docs/com_staff_wp2009_en.pdf.

[34] UN Department of Economic and Social Affairs Population Division. International Migration Report 2002, 2002. http://www.un.org/esa/population/publications/ittmig2002/2002ITTMIGTEXT22-11.pdf.

[35] Declaration of Principles – Building the Information Society: a global challenge in the new Millennium, December 2003. http://www.itu.int/wsis/docs/geneva/official/dop.html.

[36] Directorate-General of the UNESCO. Information for All Programme (AFP), 2011. http://www.unesco.org/new/en/communication-and-information/intergovernmental-programmes/information-for-all-programme-ifap/.

[37] Ford Motor Company. Fact Sheet: Ford SYNC Voice-Controlled Communications and Connectivity System, 2012. http://media.ford.com/article_display.cfm?article_id=33358.

[38] Government of India Department of Electronics & Information Technology (DeitY), Ministry of Communication & Information Technology (MC&IT). Technology Development for Indian Languages, 2012. http://tdil.mit.gov.in.

[39] African Advanced Institute for Information & Communication Technology. Human Language Technologies (HLT), 2012. http://www.meraka.org.za/humanLanguage.htm.

[40] European Commission: Bureau of European Policy Advisors. Empowering people, driving change: Social Innovation in the European Union, May 2011. http://ec.europa.eu/bepa/pdf/publications_pdf/social_innovation.pdf.

[41] LT Innovate. Language Technologies: Establishing Europe's Global Market Position and Securing the Digital Single Market. An Industry Vision, November 2012. Draft. http://lt-innovate.eu.

[42] Internet World Stats: Usage and Population Statistics, 2012. http://www.internetworldstats.com/europa.htm.

[43] Bill Meisel. Microsoft's strategic vision includes ambitious technology, October 2012. http://www.meisel-on-mobile.com/2012/10/19/microsofts-strategic-vision-includes-ambitious-technology/.

[44] European Commission. European Interoperability Framework (EIF) for European public services, 2010. http://ec.europa.eu/isa/documents/isa_annex_ii_eif_en.pdf.

[45] Gartner's 2012 Hype Cycle for Emerging Technologies Identifies "Tipping Point" Technologies That Will Unlock Long-Awaited Technology Scenarios:, August 2012. http://www.gartner.com/it/page.jsp?id=2124315.

[46] Moses – Statistical Machine Translation System, 2012. http://www.statmt.org/moses/.

[47] Special Eurobarometer 366/75.2. Building the Digital Single Market – Cross border Demand for Content Services, October 2011. http://ec.europa.eu/languages/languages-of-europe/eurobarometer-survey_en.htm.

[48] Nordens Välfärdscenter. Medier för alla?, January 2012. http://www.nordicwelfare.org/News/Medier-for-alla/.

[49] *Workshop on Language Technology for Decision Support at the Fourth Swedish Language Technology Conference*, 2012. http://permalink.gmane.org/gmane.science.linguistics.corpora/15911.

[50] Nicoletta Calzolari, Nuria Bel, Khalid Choukri, Joseph Mariani, Monica Monachini, Jan Odijk, Stelios Piperidis, Valeria Quochi, and Claudia Soria. Language Resources for the Future – The Future of Language Resources, September 2011. http://www.flarenet.eu/sites/default/files/FLaReNet_Book.pdf.

[51] ELDIA: European Language Diversity for All, 2012. http://www.eldia-project.org.

[52] Timos Sellis. Open Data and LR: Directions. FLaReNet Forum, Barcelona, Spain, March 2010. http://flarenet.eu/sites/default/files/S2_Sellis_Slides.pdf.

[53] Alfred Spector, Peter Norvig, and Slav Petrov. Google's Hybrid Approach to Research. *Communications of the ACM*, 55(7):34–37, 2012. http://cacm.acm.org/magazines/2012/7/151226-googles-hybrid-approach-to-research/fulltext.

[54] META-FORUM 2012: A Strategy for Multilingual Europe. Panel discussion "Plans for LT Research and Innovation in Member States and Regions", June 2012. Videos of this panel discussion are available at http://www.meta-net.eu/events/meta-forum-2012/programme.

[55] META-NET Statutes. Version 1.1, September 2012. http://www.meta-net.eu/META-NET-Statutes.pdf.

[56] META-TRUST AISBL (Association internationale sans but lucratif), September 2012. http://www.meta-trust.eu.

[57] European Commission. Article 185 Initiatives, 2012. http://cordis.europa.eu/fp7/art185/.

[58] European Commission. Proposal for a Regulation of the European Parliament and of the Council establishing Horizon 2020 – The Framework Programme for Research and Innovation (2014-2020), 2011. http://eur-lex.europa.eu/LexUriServ/LexUriServ.do?uri=COM:2011:0809:FIN:en:PDF.

[59] Aljoscha Burchardt, Georg Rehm, and Felix Sasaki. The Future European Multilingual Information Society – Vision Paper for a Strategic Research Agenda, 2011. http://www.meta-net.eu/vision/reports/meta-net-vision-paper.pdf,

[60] Aljoscha Burchardt, Georg Rehm, and Felix Sasaki. LT 2020. Vision and Priority Themes for Language Technology Research in Europe until the Year 2020. Towards the META-NET Strategic Research Agenda, 2012. http://www.meta-net.eu/vision/reports/LT2020.pdf.

[61] Georg Rehm and Hans Uszkoreit. Multilingual Europe: A challenge for language tech. *MultiLingual*, 22(3):51–52, April/May 2011.

LIST OF KEY CONTRIBUTORS

The experts listed in the following contributed to this Strategic Research Agenda (54% from language technology user or provider industries, 46% from language technology research, 4% from national or international institutions). The Strategic Research Agenda is presented by the META Technology Council.

1. Sophia Ananiadou, U. of Manchester, UK
2. Sanne Andresen, Ordbogen, DK
3. Toni Badia, Barcelona Media, ES
4. Antonio Balvet, U. of Lille, FR
5. Michaela Bartelt, Electronic Arts, GER/USA
6. Christoph Bauer, ORF, AT
7. Matthias Bärwolff, Tazaldoo, GER
8. Caterina Berbenni-Rehm, Promis, LUX
9. Juanjo Bermudez, Lingua e-Solutions SL, ES
10. Henriette Edvarda Berntsen, Tansa, NO
11. Nozha Boujemaa, INRIA, FR
12. Hervé Bourland, IDIAP, CH
13. Antonio Branco, U. of Lisbon, PT
14. Andrew Bredenkamp, acrolinx, GER
15. Anton Bregar, PL
16. Gerhard Budin, U. of Vienna, AT
17. Axel Buendia, Spir. Ops, FR
18. Paul Buitelaar, DERI, IE
19. Aljoscha Burchardt, DFKI, GER
20. Will Burgett, Intel, USA
21. Johannes Bursch, Daimler AG, GER
22. Miriam Butt, U. of Konstanz, GER
23. Nicoletta Calzolari, Consiglio Nazionale delle Ricerche, IT
24. Nick Campbell, Trinity College Dublin, IE
25. Olga Caprotti, U. of Gothenburg, SE
26. Jean Carrive, INA, FR
27. Khalid Choukri, ELDA, FR
28. Philipp Cimiano, U. of Bielefeld, GER
29. Ann Copestake, U. of Cambridge, UK
30. Ido Dagan, Bar-Ilan University, IL
31. Morena Danieli, Loquendo, IT
32. Christophe Declercq, Imperial College, UK
33. Claude de Loupy, Syllabs, FR
34. Maarten de Rijke, U. of Amsterdam, NL
35. Koenraad De Smedt, U. of Bergen, NO
36. István Dienes, HU
37. Alice Dijkstra, Nederlandse Organisatie voor Wetenschappelijk Onderzoek, NL
38. Marin Dimitrov, Ontotext, BG
39. Petar Djekic, SoundCloud, UK
40. Bill Dolan, Microsoft, USA
41. Rickard Domeij, Language Council of Sweden, SE
42. Christoph Dosch, Institut für Rundfunktechnik, GER
43. Christian Dugast, Tech2Biz, GER
44. Ray Fabri, U. of Malta, MT
45. Marcello Federico, FBK, IT
46. David Filip, Moravia, CZ
47. Dan Flickinger, Stanford Univ., USA
48. Gil Francopoulo, CNRS/LIMSI, IMMI, Tagmatica, FR
49. Piotr W. Fuglewicz, TiP, PL
50. Robert Gaizauskas, U. of Sheffield, UK
51. Martine Garnier-Rizet, CNRS/LIMSI and IMMI, FR
52. Simon Garrett, British Telecom, UK
53. Stefan Geissler, Temis, GER
54. Edouard Geoffrois, Ministry of Defense and French Nat. Research Agency, FR
55. Yota Georgakopolou, Deluxe Media, UK
56. Jost Gippert, U. of Frankfurt, GER
57. Mircea Giurgiu, U. of Cluj-Napoca, RO
58. Serge Gladkoff, Logrus International and GALA Standards Director, USA/RUS
59. Daniel Grasmick, Lucy Software, GER
60. Gregory Grefenstette, Exalead, FR
61. Marko Grobelnik, Institut "Jožef Stefan", SI
62. Joakim Gustafson, KTH Royal Institute of Technology, SE
63. Thomas Hagen, Dictatr AS, NO
64. Jan Hajic, Charles U. Prague, CZ
65. Paul Heisterkamp, Daimler AG, GER
66. Mattias Heldner, KTH Royal Institute of Technology, SE
67. Sebastian Hellmann, U. of Leipzig, GER
68. Manuel Herranz, PangeaMT, ES
69. Theo Hoffenberg, Softissimo, FR
70. Thomas Hofmann, Google, CH/USA
71. Timo Honkela, Aalto University, FI
72. Roman Jansen-Winkeln, Belingoo Media Group, LUX
73. Krzysztof Jassem, Poleng, PL
74. Keith Jeffery, Science and Technology Facilities Council, Rutherford Appleton Lab., UK
75. Richard Jelinek, PetaMem GmbH, GER
76. Kristiina Jokinen, U. of Helsinki, FI
77. Rebecca Jonson, Artificial Solutions, ES
78. John Judge, Dublin City U./CNGL, IE
79. Martin Kay, Stanford University, USA and Universität des Saarlandes, GER
80. Melih Karakulukcu, Karakulukcu Consulting, TR
81. Jussi Karlgren, Gavagai, FI
82. Marc Kemps-Snijders, Meertens Instituut, NL
83. Ilan Kernerman, K Dictionaries, IL
84. Christopher Kermorvant, A2iA, FR

G. Rehm and H. Uszkoreit (eds.), *META-NET Strategic Research Agenda for Multilingual Europe 2020*, White Paper Series, DOI: 10.1007/978-3-642-36349-8, © The Author(s) 2013

85. Simon King, U. of Edinburgh, UK
86. Philipp Koehn, U. of Edinburgh, UK
87. Maria Koutsombogera, ILSP, GR
88. Steven Krauwer, U. of Utrecht, NL
89. Verena Krawarik, APA, AT
90. Stefan Kreckwitz, Across, GER
91. Simon Krek, Institut "Jožef Stefan", SI
92. Brigitte Krenn, OFAI, AT
93. Sandra Kübler, Indiana University, USA
94. Michal Küfhaber, Skrivanek, CZ
95. Serg Kulikov, Russian Acad. of Sciences, RUS
96. Jimmy Kunzmann, EML, GER
97. Gunn Inger Lyse Samdal, U. of Bergen, SE
98. Bernardo Magnini, FBK, IT
99. Gudrun Magnusdottir, ESTeam, SE
100. Elisabeth Maier, CLS Communication, CH
101. Joseph Mariani, CNRS/LIMSI and IMMI, FR
102. Penny Marinou, Litterae Trans, GR
103. Margaretha Mazura, EMF, UK/BE
104. John McNaught, U. of Manchester, UK
105. Erhan Mengusoglu, Mantis, TR
106. Wolfgang Menzel, U. of Hamburg, GER
107. Roger Moore, U. of Sheffield, UK
108. Sukumar Munshi, Across, GER
109. Bart Noe, Jabbla, BE
110. Torbjørn Nordgård, LINGIT AS, NO
111. Jan Odijk, U. of Utrecht, NL
112. Stephan Oepen, U. of Oslo, NO
113. Karel Oliva, Czech Acad. of Sciences, CZ
114. Mehmed Özkan, Bogazici University, TR
115. Maja Pantic, Imperial College London, UK
116. Niko Papula, Mutilizer, FI
117. Alexandre Passant, DERI, IE
118. Pavel Pecina, Dublin City U./CNGL, IE
119. Manfred Pinkal, Universität des Saarlandes, GER
120. Stelios Piperidis, ILSP, GR
121. László Podhorányi, Vodafone, HU
122. Jörg Porsiel, VW, GER
123. Gabor Proszeky, Morphologic, HU
124. Artur Raczynski, European Patent Office, GER
125. Jens Erik Rasmussen, Mikroverkstedet, NO
126. Georg Rehm, DFKI, GER
127. Steve Renals, U. of Edinburgh, UK
128. Peter Revsbech, Ordbogen, DK
129. Giuseppe Riccardi, U. of Trento, IT
130. Daniel Ridings, Mikroverkstedet AS, LINGIT AS, NO
131. Eirikur Rögnvaldsson, U. of Iceland, IS
132. Philippe Rohou, ERCIM, FR
133. Günther Roscher, ICS Dr. G. Roscher GmbH, GER
134. Johann Roturier, Symantec, IE
135. Dimitris Sabatakakis, Systran, FR
136. David Sadek, Institute Telecom, FR
137. Sergi Sagàs, MediaPro, ES
138. Felix Sasaki, W3C and DFKI, GER
139. Jana Šatková, ACP Traductera, CZ
140. Maneerat Sawasdiwat, Rajamangala U. of Technology, TH
141. David Schlangen, U. of Bielefeld, GER
142. Jörg Schütz, Bioloom, GER
143. Bjørn Seljebotn, Nynodata, NO
144. Max Silberztein, Université de Franche-Comté, FR
145. Mirko Silvestrini, Rapidrad, IT
146. Ruud Smeulders, Rabo Bank, NL
147. Svetlana Sokolova, ProMT, RUS
148. Ralf Steinberger, JRC, EC, IT
149. Juan Manuel Soto, Fonetic, ES
150. Lucia Specia, U. of Sheffield, UK
151. C. M. Sperberg-McQueen, BlackMesa Technologies, USA
152. Peter Spyns, Flemish Government, BE
153. Maxim Stamenov, Bulgarian Acad. of Sciences, BG
154. Kerstin Steffen, Maravision, ES
155. Volker Steinbiss, RWTH Aachen and Accipio, GER
156. Rudi Studer, KIT, GER
157. Katerina Stuparicova, Charles U. Prague, CZ
158. Daniel Tapias, Sigma Tech, ES
159. Alessandro Tescari, Pervoice, IT
160. Lori Thicke, Translators without Borders and Lexcelera, FR
161. Gregor Thurmair, Linguatec, GER
162. Rudy Tirry, Lionbridge, BE
163. Attila Törcsvári, Arcanum Development, HU
164. Diana Trandabat, U. of A. I. Cuza, RO
165. Isabel Trancoso, INESC-ID, PT
166. Dan Tufis, Romanian Acad., RO
167. Hans Uszkoreit, DFKI and Universität des Saarlandes, GER
168. Erik van der Goot, Joint Research Center, EC, IT
169. Peggy van der Kreeft, Deutsche Welle, GER
170. Jaap van der Meer, TAUS, NL
171. René van Erk, Wolters Kluwer, NL
172. Josef van Genabith, Dublin City U./CNGL, IE
173. Arjan van Hessen, Twente U. and Telecats, NL
174. David van Leeuwen, TNO and Radboud University, NL
175. Andrejs Vasiljevs, Tilde, LV
176. Michel Vérel, VecSys, FR
177. Kjersti Drøsdal Vikøren, Standard Norge AS, NO
178. Bo Vincents, Ankiro, DK
179. Claire Waast, EDF, FR
180. Philippe Wacker, EMF, UK/BE
181. Wolfgang Wahlster, DFKI, GER
182. Alex Waibel, KIT, GER and CMU, Jibbigo, USA
183. Jürgen Wedekind, U. of Copenhagen, DK
184. André Wlodarczyk, U. of Charles De Gaulle, FR
185. Feiyu Xu, DFKI, GER
186. Annie Zaenen, U. of Stanford, USA
187. Jakub Zavrel, Textkernel, NL
188. Patricia Zimmermann, SpeechConcept GmbH, GER
189. Elie Znaty, VecSys, FR
190. Chenqing Zong, Chinese Acad. of Sciences, CN

MILESTONES AND HISTORY

The META-VISION process within META-NET started in early 2010, its main aim was to produce this Strategic Research Agenda. Hundreds of representatives from academia, industry, official institutions, policy makers, politicians, journalists and the language communities have contributed to this process (see Appendix B). In this section we give an overview of the meetings at which the SRA or important components on the way towards the SRA have been presented and discussed (key meetings marked in bold typeface). Important milestones in the process towards this SRA include five documents: the three Vision Reports prepared by the three domain-specific Vision Groups (see Figure 20, p. 82), a general Vision Paper [59], and a Priority Themes Paper [60] in which the technology visions are specified in a more concrete way. All reports, papers and discussions that took place in the process have been reflected in the Strategic Research Agenda. The documents are available online at http://www.meta-net.eu/vision.

1. FLaReNet Forum, Barcelona, Spain, Feb. 11/12, 2010
2. Language Technology Days 2010, Luxembourg, March 22/23, 2010
3. EAMT 2010, Saint-Raphael, France, May 27/28, 2010
4. theMETAnk, Berlin, Germany, June 4/5, 2010
5. Translingual Europe 2010, Berlin, Germany, June 7, 2010
6. Localization World, Berlin, Germany, June 8/9, 2010
7. Multisaund Seminar, Istanbul, Turkey, June 16-18, 2010
8. **Vision Group "Text Translation and Localisation"** (1st meeting), Berlin, Germany, July 23, 2010
9. **Vision Group "Media and Information Services"** (1st meeting), Paris, France, Sep. 10, 2010
10. **Vision Group "Interactive Systems"** (1st meeting), Paris, France, Sep. 10, 2010
11. ICT 2010, Brussels, Belgium, September 27-29, 2010
12. **Vision Group "Text Translation and Localisation"** (2nd meeting), Brussels, Belgium, Sep. 29, 2010
13. **Vision Group "Interactive Systems"** (2nd meeting), Prague, Czech Republic, Oct. 5, 2010
14. Languages and the Media 2010, Berlin, Germany, October 7, 2010
15. HLT: The Baltic Perspective, Riga, Latvia, October 7/8, 2010
16. LISA Forum Europe, Budapest, Hungary, October 13, 2010
17. **Vision Group "Media and Information Services"** (2nd meeting), Barcelona, Spain, Oct. 15, 2010
18. EFNIL 2010, Thessaloniki, Greece, Nov. 3, 2010
19. Interact Presidential Summit, Moffett Field, USA, Nov. 8-9, 2010
20. **META Technology Council** (1st meeting), Brussels, Belgium, Nov. 16, 2010
21. Language question in research: English vs. national languages?, Finnish Parliament, Helsinki, Nov. 17, 2010
22. **META-FORUM 2010: "Challenges for Multilingual Europe"**, Brussels, Belgium, Nov. 17/18, 2010
23. Oriental-Cocosda 2010, Kathmandu, Nepal, Nov. 24-25, 2010
24. The International Workshop on Spoken Language Translation (IWSLT), Paris, France, Dec. 2/3, 2010
25. Meeting of the LT Berlin working group, Berlin, Germany, Dec. 9, 2010
26. Language Technology for Multilingual Applications, European Parliament, Luxembourg, Jan. 27, 2011
27. Opening of German/Austrian W3C Office at DFKI Berlin, Berlin, Germany, Feb. 10, 2011
28. Japanese Workshop for Machine Translation, Tokyo, Japan, Feb. 23, 2011
29. Meeting of Representatives of European Language Councils, Copenhagen, Denmark, March 08, 2011
30. TRALOGY, Paris, France, March 3/4, 2011

G. Rehm and H. Uszkoreit (eds.), *META-NET Strategic Research Agenda for Multilingual Europe 2020*, White Paper Series, DOI: 10.1007/978-3-642-36349-8, © The Author(s) 2013

31. **Vision Group "Interactive Systems"** (3rd meeting), Rotterdam, The Netherlands, March 28, 2011
32. **Vision Group "Media and Information Services"** (3rd meeting), Vienna, Austria, April 1, 2011
33. Meeting of the LT Berlin working group, Berlin, Germany, April 4, 2011
34. W3C Workshop, Content on the multilingual web, Pisa, Italy, April 5, 2011
35. **Vision Group "Translation and Localisation"** (3rd meeting), Prague, Czech Republic, April 7/8, 2011
36. Attensity Forum 2011, Berlin, Germany, May 6, 2011
37. **META Technology Council** (2nd meeting), Venice, Italy, May 25, 2011
38. FLaReNet Forum, Venice, May 26-27, 2011
39. Multisaund Seminar, Bursa, Turkey, June 13-14, 2011
40. META-NET Workshop at ICANN 2011: Context in Machine Translation, Espoo, Finland, June 14, 2011
41. Speech Processing Conference, Tel Aviv, Israel, June 21-22, 2011
42. **META-FORUM 2011: "Solutions for Multilingual Europe"**, Budapest, Hungary, June 27/28, 2011
43. Media for All, London, June 29-July 1, 2011
44. EUROLAN 2011 Summer School, Cluj-Napoca, Romania, Aug. 28-Sep. 4, 2011
45. Interspeech 2011, Firenze, Italy, Aug. 28-31, 2011
46. RANLP 2011, Hissar, Bulgaria, Sep. 12-14, 2011
47. Multilingual Web Workshop, Limerick, Ireland, Sep. 21/22, 2011
48. ML4HMT Workshop at MT Summit, Xiamen, China, Sep. 19-23, 2011
49. Workshop Language Technology for a Multilingual Europe at GSCL 2011, Hamburg, Germany, Sep. 27, 2011
50. GSCL 2011: Multilingual Resources and Multilingual Applications, Hamburg, Germany, Sep. 28-30, 2011
51. **META Technology Council** (3rd meeting), Berlin, Germany, Sep. 30, 2011
52. Workshop on IPR and Metadata by META-NORD, Helsinki, Finland, Sep. 30, 2011
53. META-NET Network Meeting and General Assembly, Berlin, Germany, Oct. 21/22, 2011
54. NPLD Assembly, Eskilstuna, Sweden, Oct. 25/26, 2011
55. EFNIL 2011, London, UK, Oct. 26, 2011
56. Oriental-Cocosda 2011, Hsinchu, Taiwan, Oct. 26-28, 2011
57. SIMC 2011 International Maaya Symposium on Multilingualism in the Cyberspace, Brasilia, Brasil, Nov. 7-9, 2011
58. IJCNLP 2011, Chiang Mai, Thailand, Nov. 9-13, 2011
59. ML4HMT-11 Workshop, Barcelona, Spain, Nov. 19, 2011
60. LTC 2011, Poznan, Poland, Nov. 25-27, 2011
61. GALA Conference, Monaco, March 26-29, 2012
62. EACL 2012, Avignon, France, April 23-27, 2012
63. CESAR Roadshow Event, Sofia, Bulgaria, May 2, 2012
64. LREC 2012, Istanbul, Turkey, May 21-27, 2012
65. CESAR Roadshow Event, Bratislava, Slovakia, June 7/8, 2012
66. Multilingual Web Workshop, Dublin, Ireland, June 11, 2012
67. **META Technology Council** (4th meeting), Brussels, Belgium, June 19, 2012
68. **META-FORUM 2012: "A Strategy for Multilingual Europe"**, Brussels, Belgium, June 20/21, 2012
69. CHAT 2012 Workshop, Madrid, Spain, June 22, 2012
70. Language, Technologies and the Future of Europe, Riga, Latvia, September 21, 2012
71. Linguistic Technologies in the Research in Romania and in the Diaspora, Bucharest, Romania, September 26/27, 2012
72. CESAR Roadshow Event, Warsaw, Poland, September 27/28, 2012
73. Workshop on LT and Innovation, Oslo, Norway, October 15, 2012
74. EFNIL 2012, Budapest, Hungary, October 25/26, 2012
75. CESAR Roadshow Event, Belgrade, Serbia, October 29, 2012
76. European Languages in the Age of Technology – quo vadis?, Vilnius, Lithuania, November 14, 2012
77. Workshop The Portuguese Language in the Digital Age, Lisbon, Portugal, November 16, 2012
78. SIMC III, Conference of the Maaya World Network for Linguistic Diversity, Paris, France, November 21-23, 2012
79. Workshop A Roadmap for the Digital Survival of Maltese, Malta, November 24, 2012
80. Translating and the Computer Conference, London, UK, November 29/30, 2012

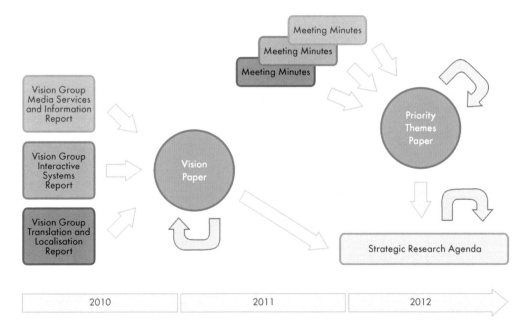

Roadmap

Strategic Research Agenda

Visions

communication to policy makers,
funding bodies, public

communication in the
wider LT Community and
among other stakeholders

communication
within META-NET (META-VISION)

| 2010 | 2011 | 2012 |

19: The three phases of the META-VISION process

Vision Group
Media Services
and Information
Report

Vision Group
Interactive
Systems
Report

Vision Group
Translation and
Localisation
Report

Meeting Minutes

Meeting Minutes

Meeting Minutes

Vision
Paper

Priority
Themes
Paper

Strategic Research Agenda

| 2010 | 2011 | 2012 |

20: Steps towards the Strategic Research Agenda for Multilingual Europe 2020

ABOUT META-NET

META-NET is a Network of Excellence partially funded by the European Commission [61]. The network currently consists of 60 members in 34 European countries. META-NET forges the Multilingual Europe Technology Alliance (**META**), a growing community of currently more than 650 language technology companies, research centres and professionals. META-NET fosters the technological foundations for a multilingual European information society that: 1. makes communication and cooperation possible across languages; 2. grants all Europeans equal access to information and knowledge regardless of their language; 3. builds upon and advances functionalities of networked information technology.

The network supports a Europe that unites as a single digital market and information space. It stimulates and promotes multilingual technologies for all European languages. These technologies support automatic translation, content production, information processing and knowledge management for a wide variety of subject domains and applications. They also enable intuitive language-based interfaces to technology ranging from household electronics, machinery and vehicles to computers and robots.

Launched on 1 February 2010, META-NET is conducting various activities in its three lines of action META-VISION, META-SHARE and META-RESEARCH. In addition, META-NET cooperates with more than 40 European projects, many research organisations, companies, language communities and industry associations.

META-VISION fosters a dynamic and influential stakeholder community that unites around a shared vision and strategic research agenda (SRA). The main focus of this activity is to build a coherent and cohesive LT community in Europe by bringing together representatives from highly fragmented and diverse groups of stakeholders. White Papers were produced for 30 languages, each one describing the status of one language with respect to its state in the digital era and existing technological support [12]. The technology vision described in this agenda was bootstrapped through three sectorial Vision Groups.

META-SHARE creates an open, distributed facility for exchanging and sharing resources. The peer-to-peer network of repositories will contain language data, tools and services that are documented with metadata and organised in standardised categories. The resources can be accessed and uniformly searched. The available resources include free, open-source materials as well as restricted, commercially available, fee-based items.

META-RESEARCH builds bridges to related technology fields. This activity seeks to leverage advances in other fields and to capitalise on innovative research that can benefit language technology. The action line focuses on conducting leading-edge research in machine translation, collecting data, preparing data sets and organising language resources for evaluation purposes; compiling inventories of tools and methods; and organising workshops and training events for members of the community.

META-VISION: Building a community with a shared vision and strategic research agenda

META-SHARE: Building an open resource exchange infrastructure

META-RESEARCH: Building bridges to neighbouring technology fields

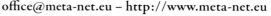

office@meta-net.eu – http://www.meta-net.eu

G. Rehm and H. Uszkoreit (eds.), *META-NET Strategic Research Agenda for Multilingual Europe 2020*, White Paper Series, DOI: 10.1007/978-3-642-36349-8, © The Author(s) 2013

MEMBERS OF META-NET

Austria	Zentrum für Translationswissenschaft, Universität Wien: Gerhard Budin
Belgium	Centre for Processing Speech and Images, University of Leuven: Dirk van Compernolle
	Computational Linguistics and Psycholinguistics Research Centre, University of Antwerp: Walter Daelemans
Bulgaria	Institute for Bulgarian Language, Bulgarian Academy of Sciences: Svetla Koeva
Croatia	Institute of Linguistics, Faculty of Humanities and Social Science, University of Zagreb: Marko Tadić
Cyprus	Language Centre, School of Humanities: Jack Burston
Czech Republic	Institute of Formal and Applied Linguistics, Charles University in Prague: Jan Hajič
Denmark	Centre for Language Technology, University of Copenhagen: Bolette Sandford Pedersen, Bente Maegaard
Estonia	Institute of Computer Science, University of Tartu: Tiit Roosmaa, Kadri Vider
Finland	Computational Cognitive Systems Research Group, Aalto University: Timo Honkela
	Department of Modern Languages, University of Helsinki: Kimmo Koskenniemi, Krister Lindén
France	Centre National de la Recherche Scientifique, Laboratoire d'Informatique pour la Mécanique et les Sciences de l'Ingénieur and Institute for Multilingual and Multimedia Information: Joseph Mariani
	Evaluations and Language Resources Distribution Agency: Khalid Choukri
	Laboratory of Computer Science, University of Le Mans: Holger Schwenk
	Laboratoire Informatique d'Avignon, University of Avignon: Georges Linares
Germany	Language Technology Lab, DFKI: Hans Uszkoreit, Georg Rehm
	Human Language Technology and Pattern Recognition, RWTH Aachen University: Hermann Ney
	Department of Computational Linguistics, Saarland University: Manfred Pinkal
	Institute for Natural Language Processing, University of Stuttgart: Jonas Kuhn, Hinrich Schütze
	Interactive Systems Lab, Karlsruhe Institute of Technology: Alex Waibel
Greece	R.C. "Athena", Institute for Language and Speech Processing: Stelios Piperidis
Hungary	Research Institute for Linguistics, Hungarian Academy of Sciences: Tamás Váradi
	Department of Telecommunications and Media Informatics, Budapest University of Technology and Economics: Géza Németh, Gábor Olaszy

G. Rehm and H. Uszkoreit (eds.), *META-NET Strategic Research Agenda for Multilingual Europe 2020*, White Paper Series, DOI: 10.1007/978-3-642-36349-8, © The Author(s) 2013

Iceland	School of Humanities, University of Iceland: Eiríkur Rögnvaldsson
Ireland	School of Computing, Dublin City University: Josef van Genabith
Italy	Consiglio Nazionale delle Ricerche, Istituto di Linguistica Computazionale "Antonio Zampolli": Nicoletta Calzolari
	Human Language Technology Research Unit, Fondazione Bruno Kessler: Bernardo Magnini
Latvia	Tilde: Andrejs Vasiļjevs
	Institute of Mathematics and Computer Science, University of Latvia: Inguna Skadiņa
Lithuania	Institute of the Lithuanian Language: Jolanta Zabarskaitė
Luxembourg	Arax Ltd.: Vartkes Goetcherian
Malta	Department Intelligent Computer Systems, University of Malta: Mike Rosner
Netherlands	Utrecht Institute of Linguistics, Utrecht University: Jan Odijk
	Computational Linguistics, University of Groningen: Gertjan van Noord
Norway	Department of Linguistic, Literary and Aesthetic Studies, University of Bergen: Koenraad De Smedt
	Department of Informatics, Language Technology Group, University of Oslo: Stephan Oepen
Poland	Institute of Computer Science, Polish Academy of Sciences: Adam Przepiórkowski, Maciej Ogrodniczuk
	University of Łódź: Barbara Lewandowska-Tomaszczyk, Piotr Pęzik
	Dept. of Comp. Linguistics and Artificial Intelligence, Adam Mickiewicz University: Zygmunt Vetulani
Portugal	University of Lisbon: António Branco, Amália Mendes
	Spoken Language Systems Laboratory, Institute for Systems Engineering and Computers: Isabel Trancoso
Romania	Faculty of Computer Science, University Alexandru Ioan Cuza of Iași: Dan Cristea
	Research Institute for Artificial Intelligence, Romanian Academy of Sciences: Dan Tufiș
Serbia	University of Belgrade, Faculty of Mathematics: Duško Vitas, Cvetana Krstev, Ivan Obradović
	Pupin Institute: Sanja Vranes
Slovakia	Ľudovít Štúr Institute of Linguistics, Slovak Academy of Sciences: Radovan Garabík
Slovenia	Jožef Stefan Institute: Marko Grobelnik
Spain	Barcelona Media: Toni Badia, Maite Melero
	Aholab Signal Processing Laboratory, University of the Basque Country: Inma Hernaez Rioja
	Center for Language and Speech Technologies and Applications, Universitat Politècnica de Catalunya: Asunción Moreno
	Department of Signal Processing and Communications, University of Vigo: Carmen García Mateo
	Institut Universitari de Lingüística Aplicada, Universitat Pompeu Fabra: Núria Bel
Sweden	Department of Swedish, University of Gothenburg: Lars Borin

Switzerland	Idiap Research Institute: Hervé Bourlard
Turkey	Tübitek Bilgem: Mehmet Ugur Dogan
UK	School of Computer Science, University of Manchester: Sophia Ananiadou
	Institute for Language, Cognition and Computation, Center for Speech Technology Research, University of Edinburgh: Steve Renals
	Research Institute of Informatics and Language Processing, University of Wolverhampton: Ruslan Mitkov
	Department of Computer Science, University of Sheffield: Rob Gaizauskas

About 100 language technology experts – representatives of the countries and languages represented in META-NET – discussed and finalised the key results and messages of the White Paper Series at a META-NET meeting in Berlin, Germany, on October 21/22, 2011.

ABBREVIATIONS AND ACRONYMS

AI Artificial Intelligence

API Application Programming Interface

CALL Computer-Assisted Language Learning

CAT Computer-Aided Translation

CEF Connecting Europe Facility

CMS Content Management System

EFNIL European Federation of National Institutions for Language

ETP European Technology Platform

GALA Globalization and Localization Association

GPS Global Positioning System

HQMT High-Quality Machine Translation

HLT Human Language Technology

HTML Hypertext Markup Language

IaaS Infrastructures as a Service

IR Information Retrieval

ISO International Organization for Standardization

ICT Information and Communication Technology

IT Information Technology

JTI Joint Technology Initiative

LR Language Resource

LSP Language Service Provider

LT Language Technology

META Multilingual Europe Technology Alliance

ML Machine Learning

MT Machine Translation

NLP Natural Language Processing

NPLD Network to Promote Linguistic Diversity

PaaS Platforms as a Service

PHP PHP: Hypertext Preprocessor

PPP Public-Private Partnership

RSS RDF Site Summary; Really Simple Syndication

SME Small and Medium Enterprises

SaaS Software as a Service

SRA Strategic Research Agenda

TFEU Treaty of the Functioning of the European Union

TM Translation Memory

TMS Translation Management System

WWW World Wide Web

W3C World Wide Web Consortium

G. Rehm and H. Uszkoreit (eds.), *META-NET Strategic Research Agenda for Multilingual Europe 2020*, White Paper Series, DOI: 10.1007/978-3-642-36349-8, © The Author(s) 2013

Printed by Publishers' Graphics LLC
DBT130429.15.17.73